Like Fathers, Like Sons:
Portraits of Intimacy and Strain

by Thomas J. Cottle

MODERN SOCIOLOGY:
A Series of Monographs, Treatises, and Texts

Edited by
GERALD M. PLATT

LIKE FATHERS, LIKE SONS: PORTRAITS
OF INTIMACY
AND STRAIN

by Thomas J. Cottle,
Harvard Medical School

ABLEX Publishing Corporation
Norwood, New Jersey 07648

Library of Congress Cataloging in Publication Data

Cottle, Thomas J.
  Like fathers, like sons.

  (Modern sociology)
  1. Fathers and sons. 2. Conflict of generations.
3. Family—United States. I. Title. II. Series.
HQ756.C68   306.8'7   81-2171
ISBN 0-89391-054-6 (C)   AACR2
ISBN 0-89391-087-2 (PBK)

Printed in the United States of America

Ablex Publishing Corporation
355 Chestnut Street
Norwood, New Jersey 07648

For Maurice H. Cottle,
my father, with love

BOOKS BY THOMAS J. COTTLE

Time's Children: Impressions of Youth

The Abandoners: Portraits of Loss, Separation and Neglect

The Prospect of Youth: Contexts for Sociological Inquiry

The Voices of School: Educational Issues Through Personal Accounts

Out of Discontent: Visions of the Contemporary University (with Craig R. Eisendrath and Laurence Fink)

Black Children, White Dreams

The Present of Things Future: Explorations of Time in Human Experience (with Stephen L. Klineberg)

A Family Album: Portraits of Intimacy and Kinship

Perceiving Time: An Investigation with Men and Women

Busing

Children in Jail

Barred from School

Black Testimony

Psychotherapy: Current Perspectives (with Phillip Whitten)

College: Reward and Betrayal

Private Lives and Public Accounts

Adolescent Psychology: Contemporary Perspectives

Human Adjustment (with Phillip Whitten)

Children's Secrets

Hidden Survivors: Portraits of Poor Elderly Jews

Getting Married (with Cathy Stein Greenblat)

Like Fathers, Like Sons

Contents

I would like to thank first and most importantly all the fathers and sons (as well as mothers and daughters) whose voices are heard in this book.

Let me thank too, my colleagues at the Harvard Medical School and Columbia College in Chicago.

In addition, special thanks must go to Sally Makacynas, William Phillips, Stephen Graubard, Mariana Fitzpatrick, Anne and Martin Peretz, Arthur Herzberg, MaryAnn Lash, Jon Dahl, Lucia Read, Marie Brown, Eliot Liebow, Viviette Reynell, Dieter Pevsner, Ray Bentley and Rosemary Daniels.

Finally, this book exists because of the extraordinary efforts of two remarkable people: My friend and editor, Professor Gerald M. Platt, and, as always, my wife, Kay Cottle.

Tom Cottle
January, 1981

Introduction

There is, I believe, a tendency shared by those of us who undertake social science research. The tendency, put simply, is to believe that the topics we choose to investigate coincide with the major concerns of those we study—or indeed of our entire society. One can see why this would be. If we, as researchers, put out such enormous energy in the pursuit of our interests, then surely everybody is as involved in our work as we, or at least as fascinated.

In truth, it is not necessarily a common occurrence for those we study to be utterly enthralled by the focus of our research as we seem to be. How many times I have experienced my own enthusiasm being deflated by the very persons whose lives generated that enthusiasm in the first place. When undertaking research, there can be no more discouraging moment. Almost to protect myself against this possibility, therefore, I have adopted a rather peculiar psychological stance; namely, I sometimes try not to reveal even to myself what the main focus of my research might be, at least in the beginning. So, I continue to tell people, which is true, that my concern for them hovers around the ways they and their families lead their lives. In this way, I neither drive the research too quickly in any particular direction, nor do I lay myself open to possible premature discouragement. With an (ideally) open-ended observational or descriptive approach, I am happy to accept whatever comes, that is, whatever a person chooses to share with me about his or her life.

As I say, the research policy may well be sound. But I must stress at the outset that part of the policy is motivated by the fear of discovering that my concern is of little interest to the people I invite to join me in the research. That I really don't know every moment what it is I hunt for, then, is in great measure an honest statement about my work. Yet below the surface of the statement lies another truth: If one goes again and again to families manifestly to learn of the ways life is led, then surely one will hardly be surprised to hear people speaking a great deal about family relationships, or, more generally, family matters. Quite probably, it is the matters of family business that intrigue me most consistently. I am not certain, actually, that I was fully aware of this interest, but over the course of doing research for fifteen years, it has become more than obvious that family matters constitute the heart of my research activities.

Now at last to the point. To discuss family matters is to focus on a great many, possibly even an infinite variety of, issues, principles, notions, problems, or what we might call "living family data." Above all, when we think of the family, we think of a set of arrangements, human arrangements among people, even if the people involved in the arrangement did not in fact create or describe the events and rituals governing the human arrangement that constitutes their own relationship, or friendship, or perhaps lack of friendship. In general terms, families are in part described by a set of relationships between people of the same age, as well as people of different ages—in some cases, moreover, people of very different ages. They are also described by a set of relationships among and between people of the same sex and of different sexes. All of this is painfully obvious. What is the family, after all, besides a collection of boys, girls, men and women, known to each other as cousin, aunt, uncle, grandmother, grandfather, son, daughter, father, mother? But notice already, as these words come into play, that feelings generated by them also come into play. To say the word "man" causes one reaction in us, to say the word "father" or "son" evokes something else, and this something else usually has a fair amount of feeling attached to it. In great measure, this book attempts to get at some of these more intensely felt aspects of family relationships in but one major sphere of those human arrangements we call family life—namely, the arrangements encompassing fathers and sons.

The truly comprehensive study of the family would examine in depth all the various bonds between and among family members. In this book we have selected one—perhaps later volumes will examine others. But one point that must be stressed now is this: A study of fathers and sons hardly could leave out mothers and daughters and sisters. It may appear, in other words, that this volume is "for men only," but that is as erroneous as a notion that men's lives alone constitute the stuff of family. A second point to be underscored, in a sense, has already been suggested. We said earlier that people do not necessarily create or define the very arrangements governing their relationships with people as close and significant to them as their own fathers and sons. We may believe that the relationships in which we find ourselves, for good or for bad, are strictly our own doing (and in some cases, sadly, undoing), but this is not the case. Cultures, religions, one's ethnicity, one's position in a society, factors of power, a range of factors, actually, may determine or shape the way families arrange human relationships. It is not insignificant to mention in this regard, moreover, that the very names boys and men may use in speaking or referring to one another, while revealing a certain degree of intimacy or strain, quite probably are chosen from among a list that the culture in its way offers. Every one of these words, moreover, has attending to it an almost tangible slice of feeling. The words, "my dad," connotes one thing when a boy utters these words to another boy. Something else is communicated in "my old man." Do sons still call their fathers Pop? Or Papa? Think of a letter commencing: Dear Dad. Or, Dearest Father. Personal feelings, to be sure, are expressed in these mere appellations, but let us not forget that people "turn" to their cultures for the assortment of labels and styles of interacting, and, in their way, make their conscious and unconscious selections.

The overriding theme of this book is the relationship between fathers and sons, and, as the table of contents indicates, one of the subthemes, often forgotten, is that of father *as* son. But let me quickly reassert that consciously it was not my intention to write such a book. The entire project seemed to unfold, or emerge, without me seemingly making it happen. Over the years, no matter what I worked on, the imagery of sons and fathers reappeared. Naturally, at times I talked to young men about their fathers. I spoke as well with older men about *their* fathers and of course their sons. In the main, the world painted by a son, say, was fairly close to that world as his father painted it, but often, I found, it was remarkable how little the two men knew of each other's lives. Still, the finding hardly surprised me. Indeed the thing that surprised me was that I never focused directly on fathers and sons but went on for years writing about various fathers' descriptions of their lives and various sons' descriptions of *their* lives. The "discovery" that from numerous perspectives and with wholly different intentions, a larger work was beginning to take shape, a work devoted directly to fathers and sons, dawned much later.

But now a word of clarification, if not an open disclaimer. The two scintillating words, fathers and sons, already begin to connote more than originally we may intend. To say, for example, that I am a son is to directly tie my identity to my mother and father. (Interestingly though, to be a son usually implies being the son of a mother more than a father.) To say that I am a father implies that my identity is tied rather directly to my children. To say that I am a man has the effect of loosening my ties to members of any generation. Obviously the word "man" implies a host of meanings and evokes a great many feelings, but for me it always makes me think of that medical illustration of the naked man standing somewhat dumbly, his arms hanging loose at his sides, palms turned slightly open. That is not, however, the picture I imagine when the words father and son flash before my eyes.

I have offered these brief remarks at the outset for several reasons. First, a word of explanation seemed in order given the anthology nature of the book. Quite likely the reader might wonder just what are all these various "studies" doing between the same covers. Second, I felt it important to at least hint at the fact that the material to be covered in this book is aimed as much at affecting the reader's sensibilities as it is at informing him or her about the nature of the father–son association. Said differently, if social scientists legitimately speak of survey data, laboratory data or experimental data, then in this volume we are "working with" or considering human data. There has been no special experimental intervention undertaken in this work; nor have we outlined a series of questions to be put to a randomly sampled group of sons and fathers. Instead, we have attempted to follow a small group of men, young and old, through the course of their lives and take from them relatively small passages of their words in which they speak directly or indirectly about father and son relationships. Doing what has been called "life studies" in this rather indirect and seemingly catch-as-catch-can manner may seem wholly unsystematic, but this volume may give the reader an answer to why some social scientists operate in this rather unpredictable and unscientific (in natural scientific terms) manner.

Everyone knows that during the day one sees an object looked at head on, as well as objects "trapped" in the peripheral field of vision. Similarly, one learns that at night this normal description of vision breaks down. When scant light aids our vision, we look not directly at the object but slightly away from where we know it will be. Peripheral vision, simultaneously, is all but lost, and we wander about with our head tilted in a peculiar fashion doing our best to "focus" on the imagined penumbra of an object rather than on the object itself. Whereas even the young child learns this night vision of seeing, it almost never becomes a fully automatic process. So used are we to peering straight on at an object, that night time vision takes a few moments of concentration and accommodation. Whereas some of the accommodation is physiologically and anatomically determined, some of it depends on our having to remind ourselves that we might again adapt our night time mode of seeing.

The reason for all the head cocking has to do with the location of rods, cones, a blind spot in the retina where the optic nerve enters the eye, and a host of other fascinating matters that for better or worse need not concern us here. Instead, it is a metaphor and an analogy that we want to pursue. Specifically, the cocking of the head to one side, like the sighted actor attempting to appear that he or she is blind (for in truth the blind do not do this as often as sighted people imagine that they do), is what some of us do in undertaking our research. At times we look to the penumbra of the persons we study so that the persons will not feel self-conscious about our keeping our eye on them. After all, an examination of another person in which that person is asked to speak about the way he or she leads his or her life would surely cause that person to keep his or her own eyes focused inward. And do we not watch ourselves watching ourselves during the highly self-conscious act of listening to someone, or revealing even fragments of our lives to another person! So we as researchers avoid looking dead on in order to not make already self-conscious people (that is, people we have asked to become intentionally self-conscious) uncomfortably self-conscious.

We look away for other reasons as well. Sometimes, as I mentioned earlier, it is because we honestly do not know what it is we would do best to look at
in the first place. We look away so that the other person will not read some
unintended expression on our face and thereby be conditioned to believe that
certain topics are to be mined, while other topics are to be considered insignificant or taboo. We look away at times in order to hide our own self-
consciousness. One thing more: We often look away in order to inspect the
material, literal, emotional, and spiritual that surrounds the words we are hearing
and the sights that we are directly perceiving. Given the topic that we are
addressing in this book, it is evidence that there are a great deal of valuable,
touching, informative, and utterly human factors in the expressions of men
addressing the topic of themselves as sons and/or fathers. One might say there is
inevitably more in any conversation than that which meets the ear or eye. Certainly this is true in the following accounts. But note that when I point this out, I
do not intend to speak merely as the outside observer or witness. It is not only I
the observer and witness bearing testimony to this richness. This more than meets
the ear and eye richness of the father–son bond; it is the speaker himself. For in
every account heard in the following pages, the reader will recognize an accounting as well. That is, as the person himself or herself tells his or her story, built
into the story is the teller's own interpretation of the story. While our own
interpretations and notions are compressed in the final chapter, the reader should
not be misled to believe that *all* one hears in the accounts is the particular story;
all human beings only naturally proffer their interpretations as they offer their
accounts.

In the past I have repeatedly argued that when one undertakes life study
research, one is interested only in a single person's account and accounting. No
one speaks for anyone but himself or herself, I have written elsewhere, so often
in fact that I almost came to believe the notion myself. Now I remain uncertain.
Granted, no two fathers, or sons, or men, or father–son associations are identical;
human evolution precludes this from happening. But is it the case that not even
one universal element of life is contained in the single life? Are there not aspects
of the father-ness, or son-ness, that all men experience? Is it merely the researcher's dream that he or she will find in the idiosyncratic life story truths that are
built upon universal principles, universal givens? Truthfully, I cannot be certain.
A part of me says my life is wholly my own; indeed it is the only thing that is my
own and hence I cannot share the same space or time with another man or
woman. Not my father, not my son. Another part of me says in everyone's life I
see, feel, hear, sense, or *choose* to see, feel, hear, sense pieces of my own life,
and thus I can be joined to another's life in the act or transaction which is nothing
more, nothing less than an encounter of our mutual presences. Significantly, I
can encounter another life through reading about it, just as I can by holding a
conversation with another person. In this encounter, one philosophy teaches me
that all moments of all time are conjoined, as are all lives. There is, in other

words, a concrescence of individual beings taking place in the single encounter, and, hence, in the story that is told by one individual to another. This last point, incidentally, must not be minimized as we prepare to turn to the following chapters. Expressions, utterances, pieces of life stories surely are what we are addressing, or should I say encountering. But they are not expressions or stories told to a void. They are words taken from conversations, from human encounters where, to repeat, individual lives have met. In this particular instance, moreover, the stories of all the men heard in this book were told to me, so one could argue that the form of encounter to which I too contributed, not to mention what for a variety of reasons I chose to reproduce from literally hundreds of hours of conversation, also shape the stories. These matters, too, must be considered in assessing the method of inquiry employed in the studies and the quality of truth generated in them.

But note the more significant point: the encounter, and, more precisely, the inevitability of the encounter not only between researcher and subject, but in this volume, between subject and his father and/or son. In the studies that we now address, everyone necessarily speaks to and about "that other person" as he exists in the real world, that other person as he exists in the mind of the subject, and that other person as he exists in an actual or imagined encounter. At any and all times, these three levels of human experience are operating, along with, or perhaps even embedded in the encounter of the researcher and his subject.

Finally, there is that matter again of whether "all" encounters of fathers and sons are embedded in these encounters. It is more than a philosophical conundrum; it is really a social psychological reality that all people must work out as they attempt to devise a sense of their own identity. For one's identity is produced in part by, just as it further shapes human encounters, both real and imagined. Because we encounter so much, and so many, and live with the possibility of imagining any and all encounters, it would seem only natural that the bond between father and son, or the most profound definition of a man as father and/or son, should forever contain not merely the most primitive and sophisticated layers of a human association, but the most wide sweeping, perhaps even universal, features of a human association. And one final matter to note here: we say human associations, not simply male or masculine associations. As the late Flannery O'Connor reminded us, all of us are part of a *human* drama, and thus we share the facts as well as the modes of life with all people, not merely the people of our sex, social standing, ethnic, or religious involvements or commitments. We even share the drama with, which means we encounter, people of all ages. And because we have either been that age, or find it possible to imagine ourselves that age, the universals of the life cycle necessarily color our conceptions of ourselves as people, fathers, sons, whatever.

In the end, I embark on a consideration of fathers and sons with an overwhelming uncertainty about a great number of factors, some of which, hopefully, will be clarified by the time we reach the concluding pages of this work. The task now is to permit ourselves to encounter the encounters being presented in the following portraits. Hopefully, each individual study as well as the accumulation of materials represented by their combined weight illuminates not merely the human association described by the mutual presences of fathers and sons, but all human associations, presently ongoing, remembered, and most assuredly imagined.

___1___

The First Child to Go to College

On the corner of Cheshire and McNulty Streets in Somerville, Massachusetts, stands a simple gray wood house. On the west side of the house is a glorious elm tree, its branches hanging over the eaves of the second floor. The neighbors say the tree is one of the oldest in Somerville but that it is only a matter of time before it will be hit by the disease that shortens the life of this elegant species. Still it hangs on, seemingly untouched by illness or, for that matter, by the course of history.

Twenty-six years ago, and just beyond his thirty-second birthday, Emil Morosco bought the gray house on the corner of Cheshire and McNulty Streets and moved his bride, Sarah, and their two small children into its seven comfortable rooms. The corner location made it a special house, Emil's parents said. The elm tree was an important omen, even if the weeds in the small yard were a bit of a nuisance. The house was a financial risk, but with a veteran's loan and a good job in a construction firm, there was little fear of Emil Morosco's not meeting his mortgage and insurance payments. Sarah could always do part-time work, and the boys, although small children now, would someday be wage earners themselves. According to the American dream, a man's goal should be to have a job, own a house, earn enough to keep his wife from having to work, and have a bunch of children. The house on the corner was a beginning.

The years passed calmly for the Moroscos. The two boys grew beautifully, and two more sons were born in the 1950s. Emil's job remained secure, and gradually he began to think of retirement. There was talk of buying a small cabin in New Hampshire for summer trips. A new car was hardly an every year affair, but no one can remember the Morosco's owning any one car for longer than four

1

years. Despite rises in prices and property taxes, the Moroscos were managing. Always there was the house on the corner and the friends advising Emil and Sarah to hold on to it; they could live their entire old age on the equity it would bring.

To hear the Moroscos recount the last twenty-five years is to bear witness to the turns of history. It is an ascent Emil speaks of when he reflects on his own development. His parents were born in the old country in Castelbuono near Palermo and as far as anyone can tell never attended school. Sarah's father died soon after her birth, leaving her mother with no money. Both families had come to Boston and eventually moved to Somerville. Emil's father, Guido, worked in road construction and spent the major part of his life pushing granite curbstones into place with thick iron rods. A grueling job usually given to Italians and Portugese, it left him with a crippled back and an arthritis in his neck that tortured him until his death on Christmas Eve 1965.

Emil had taken the steps his father had wanted for him. He completed two years of high school before entering the army. Education was the most important project, his father had always told him. "Have your sons go to school. They can never go enough. Don't let them stop. You can always earn money, but you can't always get the 'proper education.' " Soon after his first two grandsons were born, Guido Morosco purchased two one-hundred-dollar bonds. "Money for education," he told his son. "Government money for education. It's better than gold." Emil recalls wondering whether he should tell his father that with public education the boys did not need extra money for school. "The state pays," he wanted to tell his father, but he thought better of it. Besides, it was a lot of money and there was no reason to hurt the elder Morosco's feelings.

It was not for grammar school and high school, however, that Guido Morosco had started his little education fund. It was college he had in mind. Often he would walk about the campuses of Harvard and Boston University dreaming of the day when a grandson of his might attend one of these schools. He dreamed too of his own father, buried in Tortorici, and what the old man might have thought had he known his great-grandson might graduate from college in America. For generations no one by the name of Morosco had ever gone to school, and suddenly, in the movement of a single generation, there would be two boys, maybe dozens of boys attending *college*!

"It was his dream," Emil Morosco told me in January 1974. "First, the house. Poppa had such a thing about this house, and the tree. I think he'd have shot anybody coming even to look at the tree. But education was his highest priority. That's what he always talked about. He used to have a saying about how you could always tell an uneducated man, no matter how high he worked his way up. I never understood his dream about college, about sending at least one of my sons to college. When he put those bonds away for them, I thought he meant high school, but it was college. Even then.

"When you don't have anything, and you come from the old country, like both my parents did, the first thing you worry about is work. When I came back from the war, Poppa could see that employment wasn't the serious problem anymore. Then, when we bought the house, that convinced him it was time we moved up, in the society at large, I mean. I'd always believed that ownership was the main thing. When a man moved from an apartment to a house, he had moved in more ways than one. You get what I mean? But my father thought the way to move was through education. I never saw it that way because college was for rich families, not families like ours. Even when we moved and the boys were doing well in school, I still didn't think college was part of the plan. They'd finish high school—not like their old man—and if the army didn't get them, they'd go to work. Maybe they'd stay home a few years with their parents, maybe not. But college? You had to have money for college."

"But there were lots of families," I reminded him, "who didn't have much money who got their kids to college."

"You think it wasn't mainly for the rich?" Emil questioned me sharply.

"I agree, it was essentially, and certainly originally for the rich," I said. "But not *every* family with a kid in college was rich."

"But it wasn't only the money. It was what they call a life style. I knew about public colleges. What the hell, in my business I'd done work for some of the colleges. I talked with fellows there, you know, so I understood what it was all about. But I had this idea you sent your kids to college either if you had a lot of money or no money at all. You know what I mean? People like us, people in between, we sent our kids to high school, that was all. It was the life style. I mean, what kind of clothes do they wear at college? And what kinds of people do they meet there? I don't mean political types, I mean, who do they *meet* there? They go to school with Mr. Rockefeller's sons, or Mr. Kennedy's sons? You know what I mean? I had to ask myself those questions."

Emil saw me nodding, apparently in agreement, but he must have detected a peculiar look on my face.

"You don't see the serious part of this, but it's shaky for me to think about this. I used to wonder, what if one of my kids goes, let's say, to Boston College. That's a reasonable place, OK? Not Harvard, something at our level. And let's even say that he does fine. Then one night comes a knock on the door and there he is, you know what I mean, with a girl. Someone from the college too. Now, how do we know she fits in? Or maybe I should say, how do we know we're *up* to her expectations? With the way they dress at college you can't tell rich kids from poor kids, except the rich speak differently. For God's sake, I could have the daughter of some New York banker standing right over there in that doorway looking at the way we live.

"See, what I hadn't worked out for myself was that *I* wasn't ready to be part of the college business. Get what I'm driving at? My kids were ready, but I was the guy who had to get prepared. It didn't fit in with what I thought we were in the society at large. Look, this week begins 1974. I got a father, had a father," he corrected himself, "who never went to school, *grade* school, and I'm waiting around to see which college is going to accept my son. In a few years we go from nothing to having a choice. It's only a few years. It's not easy to get ready. It takes an adjustment. My son has to make an adjustment; I have to too."

"What about Sarah? Does she have to make an adjustment too?" I smiled.

"Sarah's already in college." Emil grinned with more than a trace of pride. "She loves that Michael's applying. As far as she's concerned, he's a college man. You know what it is with me? It's a feeling that even though I know I'm doing something right—I mean, you don't argue with the idea of your kid going to college—maybe I'm also doing something wrong. I keep telling myself it's good, it's important. Maybe I feel I'll be left behind, maybe that's it. I'm willing to consider that as a possibility. But it's more than that. College is sacred. It's like the church. You take your hat off in church, and you whisper, you know what I mean? It's sacred. You go there, you have to have special feelings, you have to think special kinds of thoughts. It's the best the society has to offer. It's not like a job or a place you go for a vacation. It's a serious thing, going to college. It's sacred, like I say."

"But Emil," I interrupted, "anybody can go to church."

"Well, then that makes college even more sacred because not everybody can go. Lots of people, like me until a few years ago, we didn't think of sending our children to college. It wasn't a possibility for us. 'Course, lots of people do it automatically. The second the child is born they're moving around getting them set up in the best colleges."

"But Michael's going to go," I stated firmly.

"If the Lord smiles on us, he'll go. He'll go to a public school, but he's dead set on going."

"And you support him." I practically gave him no alternative.

"You bet I do. I got it in perspective now. It's the most important step a person can take. It's what separates people in this society. More than money. If you really want to divide this country into the haves and the have-nots, you ask them one question: 'Did you go to college?' You take a person that earns a million dollars a year who never went to college, you'll find out the minute he opens his mouth. You can see it on television when they interview some guy. The second he speaks, you know if he went to college."

"And if he did?"

"He sounds finer, more refined. More cultured, sophisticated, man of the world. Intelligent. It's all the same thing. He sounds better, that's all."

"And that means that you . . ."

Emil cut me off. "That means I sound less educated than my son. And if you hear us talking you know goddamn well that he sounds more intelligent. He'll be a man of the world compared to me. I've got the corner lot here, but he'll move out of Somerville soon, maybe out of this state in a few years. Maybe out of the country too, for that matter. A college education, there's no telling where he'll end up. Education puts surprises and mysteries in a person's life; working nine to five takes all the surprises and mysteries out of your life. You know what I mean?''

Anyone listening to the conversations in the Morosco home during the winter of 1974 would have heard uncertainty in Emil's words. Clearly, there was a lingering tension about his son's admission to college, but there was never the feeling that he was supporting an improper development. Nor was he afraid of some brewing competition with his son, a progression on the part of the younger man by which Emil would feel intimidated. The prospect of his son's admission, for the while, was shaking his sense of social position. Never had I heard him use the phrase ''in the greater society'' as often as during those winter conversations. The thought of college had changed his perspective. He was a man turning on a wheel, expecting any minute to come out of the shadows and face the sun head on. In effect, he was watching himself watching himself, that familiar act of self-assessment one experiences when one's sense of security has been challenged. Emil Morosco could speak of his own advancement, but the ascent was described somehow from afar, as though he were looking back and saying, ''I've come a long way.'' Rarely did he describe himself living in the precise moment of promotion or achievement. He merely used past positions, salaries, and residences as benchmarks of advancement; he knew, now in his middle years, that he was beyond these points.

With Michael about to enter college, however, Emil saw himself smack in the middle of tangible mobility; he was feeling his movement in ''the greater society'' as it was happening. On several occasions he even asked me whether I noticed any physical changes about him. I remarked that waiting and worrying sometime make people age faster. ''Not that at all,'' he corrected me. ''I'm moving up in the world. If anything, I should be looking younger, and more proud. They aren't going to be able to take this one away from me. Bunch of the fellows where I work have kids in college, but it still isn't the expected way. Getting a kid into college is still a serious event for the people I work with. You shouldn't be seeing age in my face. That's a little elegance growing there. Huh? What do you say to *that*?''

Official announcement of Michael's admission to the university came in late March. The Moroscos dined out several nights in a row to celebrate. For six months, Emil Morosco had secretly put money away for just this moment. The first night they went to their favorite restaurant in Chelsea. On the second night, amid protests from his family, Emil chose a downtown Boston Hotel dining room. He insisted that his family dress up and that Michael invite one of his girl friends. Emil told his wife, ''I'd like the chance to be able to say in my way that I'm ready for this, that I can live like I think a person should who's sending a kid to college. It's a day of major change. Close your eyes, you'll feel the ground shift. Something about this generation thing,'' he whispered, ''it's really true. The kids finally take you with them. You take them through high school, but they take you the rest of the way. What we're celebrating is not just Michael being a man. We're celebrating changes in both our manhoods. I'm a better man for what he's achieved. He boosts me up now; we boost each other. We're going to celebrate because my father would have wanted us to.

"This is the second of the three big changes in an immigrant family's life." He winked at his son as though at last the younger man would fully appreciate his philosophy. "The first step is taken by the grandfather. He comes from the old country and plants roots, good roots. Then his son establishes himself as a *real* American, which means educating his children, educating them all the way. Michael goes to college. Number three is the time when you really arrive, not in the country, but in the greater *society*." He faced his son. "This change is yours, and I pray to the Almighty that I can see that day like your grandfather would have wanted to see you this night. When your child goes to college, which ought to be practically automatic, you got to pay for him. Send him to a private school, scholarship or no. 'Cause when you've got one kid in private school, you *know* you've got real earning power and that means you've got the country working for you instead of the other way around. Then you're a real insider. Then you're in the special clubs."

Sarah looked at her two men with a pride I had never seen in her before. Emil, too, seemed satisfied, as much by his speech as by his son's accomplishment. Michael, however, looked puzzled. "That's your theory, Dad?" he asked.

"That's no theory, that's facts!"

"I think you're making too much of it. Clubs and insiders? I don't want to be inside the country. I'll always be an Italian, just like you."

"You speak Italian, smarty pants?" Emil teased him.

"No, but I . . ."

"Then you're no more an Italian than Cottle here." Emil's look became stern; his deep brown eyes skipped between his son and me. There was no doubt that this was a man's issue; he never once glanced back at Sarah.

"Now look, you two," Emil began. "We celebrate tonight. Just the family. We honor our parents, the country of our parents' birth, and this country too. We have all kinds of faults to find with this country, starting with their treatment of our people. We don't forget for a minute the way my father was deprived the chance of working. We don't forget how he broke his back with those curbstones on the streets where the rich live. That you can understand. But there's a chance in this country; it just takes a while before you get it. Everybody knows immigrants have to wait in line for their visas and their entry papers. And once they're in, they wait all over again to get a job, to get a house, to get accepted. The mistake everybody makes is thinking it all comes in a lifetime. Your getting into college, my friend, comes after two lifetimes of waiting. It started one helluva long time before you were even born, and it doesn't end for at least another lifetime, with your own kid, if you think you're up for that.

"When I talk to you about clubs, I don't mean downtown clubs for famous people. I mean walking into the Ritz Carlton and having a reservation, eating nice food, wearing nice clothes, having people wait on me, bringing me things to eat. You get my point? When I can do that, then I'm in the society, and no matter what anybody tells you, the password is college. Without it you're nothing. Until that day, everybody spots you as what they call a self-made man. But you're going to be a college-made man, and that means you're on the same level as the most powerful people in this country. You'll become a professional!'' He pointed his finger at Michael. ''You know what that means, professional? It means education. Knowledge, class, money, the best this country has.''

Obviously embarrassed, Michael wiped nervously at his nose and cheeks. ''You mean I get to end up like the president?'' he muttered.

''Don't give me tough boy talk,'' Emil admonished him. ''Education didn't ruin the president. Selfishness, greediness ruined him, not college. And who's going to get him out if it isn't the smartest men in this country. Don't be cute with me. You've got the big chance. You think winning a lottery's important? All that money isn't going to do what your diploma's going to do, if you think you're up to it. Hundred-thousand-dollar-a-year ball player? It don't impress me. Doing what you'll be doing, *that* impresses me.''

Emil was finished, but his son had one last protest. ''I won't earn in my lifetime what those guys earn in a few years.''

''I got nothing against athletes,'' Emil replied. ''But you'll have something none of 'em have. It's called durability. What are they going to do when they're thirty, forty, fifty, the majority of 'em? They'll become like me, except their stories about the past will be more exciting. While they're telling their friends pushing curbstones about how they once hit .230 for the Red Sox, you'll be moving up. They'll be coming down, you'll be moving up. And you still will when you're sixty. You'll see how brains can carry a man when his body can't, but just having brains won't do it. You got to have a diploma. You got to have a lot of what this country decides is the right kind of money. Sometimes it's plain old dollars and cents, sometimes it's credentials. You'll have it all, my boy,'' he concluded thoughtfully, ''if you work. It's there for the taking for the first time in this family's history as far back as anyone can remember. Now go comb your hair 'cause you're still my son until September and we'll celebrate. And when you graduate we'll do it again, except then *you'll* pay!''

Once again Emil Morosco looked pleased. He waited for Michael to reply, knowing the younger man had declared him the winner. How important it was in that moment for Emil to be able to triumph with words. All of us in the room recognized this. Accompanying me to the door, Emil clutched my arm and gave it a squeeze as if to remind me one last time of his physical strength. Then he looked over his shoulder at where Michael had stood. I could feel joy, unadulterated joy spreading into every cell of his body. ''How do you like that kid,'' he said loudly, ''thinking his old man's a slouch 'cause I never went to college? You think tonight's the night I should tell him I went to Harvard?'' He swung open the door and literally shoved me out into the late afternoon sun.

2

Seeing Fate
with One's
Own Eyes

In almost the exact middle of Cauley Street in Brixton, on the top floor of a tan brick row house, is a four-room flat that runs from the front of the building to the rear. The front windows overlook the street, the rear windows overlook the British Railway tracks. The flat is quiet from one in the morning until six. For the remaining hours, the racket on Cauley Street can make you believe you are living in the middle of a football stadium. The noises of people laughing, yelling, bartering, arguing, screaming for their children or merely passing the time of day is so intense, a person must forfeit any hope of hearing his or her inner voice. The world assaults you in this third-floor flat on Cauley Street, and if you somehow could block out the exterior sounds, the noise coming from the family of eight within the flat would more than make up for that exterior calm.

Frank and Miriam Delano were married in the West Indies and moved to London ten years ago. At the time they had four children. Three more children were born in England but one died from a lung illness before he left the hospital. When Frank Delano lost his job with the West Indian Postal Service, he went to live in the United States. In Connecticut he worked for a tobacco company, in New Jersey for a trucking firm, lifting crates on and off the giant trailers. He was never allowed to drive. When the New Jersey job fell through, for reasons that were never explained to him, he returned to the Islands and managed to find part-time work hauling stone for the terraces being built with the new hotels, but after a year, there was no work.

With money that Miriam's mother had saved from years of working as a chambermaid, the Delanos moved to London, more precisely to Brixton. They preferred to live elsewhere, but an information clerk at Waterloo Station where they first arrived with their four children advised them right off, and with disdain, that "their type" lived either in the district near Nottinghill Gate, or in Brixton. Studying the city's tube plan, they saw it was easier to get from Waterloo Station to Brixton than to Nottinghill Gate, and that's where they went. After ten years in the British capital, they have never visited Nottinghill Gate.

Employment opportunities in England were not as great as the Delanos had been led to believe when in the Islands. There were some jobs, however, and Frank took as many as he could, often working four jobs simultaneously. Miriam found a flat with three bedrooms on Kilmore Street and prospects loomed rather promising. They were disturbed by the London rain and cold, and particularly by the condition of the older children's school, which seemed run-down and uninspiring, but one could not complain. Millions of people in the world, they assured each other, had it far worse than they.

In time, the employment situation worsened. Soon there were only two jobs for Frank, then one, then periods of unemployment, some lasting as long as six months. And there were two more children. With money tight, and England undergoing massive economic inflation, they had no choice but to move to a flat on Cauley Street which was almost as large as the Kilmore Street flat but almost half the cost. It was noisier, too, and dirtier and more depressing. Fortunately the children could remain in the same school, but it too had continued to decline in quality, and it never had much of a reputation. Teachers were constantly leaving, and were replaced by others who were inexperienced and intolerant. The Delanos watched innumerable television documentary films and news clips on American slums, and they remarked not on the untenable conditions of America's cities, but on the untenable conditions on Cauley Street. And they listened to London politicians speaking of a race problem that England expected would surface in the next ten years.

Frank Delano is a short, powerfully built man who looks much younger than his forty-six years. He has a full head of hair and such a heavy beard that he often shaves twice a day. He values his clean appearance—clothes pressed, shoes shined, fresh handkerchief—but says his patience, which he had always believed to be his finest quality as it had been his mother's, has long since disappeared. He says too that his spirit is destroyed. If there had been any hope, any optimism about the move to England, it was broken last summer when his son Michael, who everyone calls Mikko, became one of London's many school-leavers. Advised by his teachers to quit school at the age of fifteen, Mikko eagerly set about to find employment. Offices in Brixton and in central London furnished him with lists of potential employers, but nothing materialized. Indeed, Mikko never even felt he had come close to landing a job. So with his teachers seemingly relieved to be rid of him, and his chances for employment next to nothing, he roamed London with a group of boys who spent more time playing the machines in penny arcades than anything else, until one of them, Eddie Balassi, a bloke everyone said slept in his dark brown leather coat, was arrested for breaking into a cleaning shop.

News of Eddie Balassi's arrest almost killed Frank Delano. He did not wish to accept that this was what he would find on emigrating to England. He blamed the country and the government; he spoke of the documentaries he had seen on television; but mostly he blamed the schools.

"Look about this flat," he told me, one bitter cold December afternoon, three weeks after the arrest. The noises rising up from the street were punctuated only by the rush of the trains from the rear of the building, and the room was filled with the odor of Frank Delano's aftershave cologne. "You couldn't live here," he said. "You couldn't bear to live here. Many people would have left long ago. I know that. I know that. But a person can endure it here. You wear every bit of clothing you own in the cold, and rot in the summer from the heat and the smells, but you can endure it. But let them tell me how they keep their schools so bad while the rest of London education is so superior. And I know that to be the case. I know it. I've seen those other communities. I've worked in them for ten years. But look what they provide for us. They keep us away from them, arm's length, letting my children go to school as though they were doing us a favor. They *have* to let my children go to school, and they know it, so they make the schools rotten. I know that they do. They work on it when they can. All they want is to keep the children alive until they are old enough to speak to them about leaving. You know about our famous school-leavers? How they tell children they have had enough education so they might go out and locate a job? But do you think anyone has a job for people like us? You see the prices yourself, you see the cost of living in a place as uncomfortable as this. How can they tell children that the country has jobs for them!

"Oh, I know what they want from us, I know it. I've been to the school meetings often enough to see what their officers are thinking about when they sit there looking at us. They are thinking, 'We never should have let you enter this country. We should have closed the doors when we first had a chance. We made the same mistake with the Indians and the Pakistanis. What were we thinking about when we let unskilled men arrive in this country?' But they took care of us, with our children. Mikko leave school and find a job? How could anyone take that as wise advice? A colored man in this country has his name on the bottom of every employment list, no matter what they say. Whites at the top, coloreds at the bottom. But it makes things better at the school for them. That is why they want it so. Too many children in a class, too much noise, no way to teach all the children in little rooms, no space, and the bigger ones make problems for them.

"Look at Mikko's friend, this Balassi. He's a criminal. I read about types like him. I do not associate with him. I lived my life to keep away from the Balassis. But school did it to him too. They spotted the boys who gave them trouble and told them to leave. Try, go on the train to London and look for jobs, they said. Girls too. Foolish, wasteful nonsense. And what chance did the parents of these children have with them hearing the advice of their *teachers* every day? It went through them, everything we tried to tell them. I had Mikko in here every night for three months. I told him on his fifteenth birthday that the most important act of his life was his education. But he had better ideas than his father. 'They don't do it like that here,' he told me, how many times! Where do you suppose he got these ideas, and his rudeness. From down there!'' Frank Delano swung his arm around as if he wanted to punch a hole in the window. ''And from that school of his. From that school. I know it.

''I'll tell you something, honest. Mikko is not smart enough to think up the idea of leaving school. He learned it from his teachers, he saw fate with his own eyes. He looked about that school, he looked about the schools where the rich send their children and he said to himself, 'What is my future if I stay here? What do I own at the end? I'll become like my father, wasting years, hunting for work where anyone with intelligence knows there cannot be work. And I don't want to end up like my father. I want it better.' And why shouldn't he have it better? Why should a son respect the steps of his father? Education is supposed to change that. My mother taught us that lesson forty-five years ago. No one falls upon money. A man works to find opportunities. But they sing differently now in these schools. They tell their children, go to work. That is how, don't you see, they control us, keep us in that part of the society and the part of the city where they like it best for us to be. It makes it nice for them. If Mikko finds his job, so much the better for him *and* the economy. But they know that Mikko will find nothing, I know. I know what there is for him to find. I have few skills, but I found something in my life. He has no skills, no skills. He has learned nothing in these schools. He learned as a child, in the beginning. We were excited. And he loved it. He was never late to his first school. But in the middle school we saw it changing.

''It has been this way with all the children. By the time they are nine or ten, the world closes down again, they have lost interest, the school has taught them how to lose interest, and it becomes very, very late for them. I have watched it happening with all my children. Bright babies, so much energy. And then in a few years they are changed people, as if we hadn't fed them properly, or let them have their exercise. It is the schools. They build their classes and that idea of leave-taking. Then the child fails on his own, you see what I mean, and the school can tell me, 'But it has nothing to do with us. Mikko chose to leave.' My son never chose such an action in his life. He follows orders. All the young follow orders; that is all they know. They follow orders of the television, their friends, their schools. Mainly the schools. They are being trained to see the uselessness of education. I call this a crime. It is disastrous. Eddie Balassi breaks into that store and walks right into the police. He has committed a crime and must be punished. Mikko is told to leave school, that they will find a place for him in the world, and anyway, they will take him back. All that is also a crime. But he does not walk into the police. It is worse for him, because he walks into nobody. No one is anywhere to help him or advise him. It would be better if a policeman found him and told him where he should be going. They stopped me and they will stop Mikko, then all his brothers and sisters.

"The test of the society is the schools, and our schools here are no better than what I knew. Maybe they are worse. This is a horrible admission, to myself, to realize that what I have tried to do in my life has brought me and seven other people just to this. There are times, you know, when I cannot bear the thought of it. I feel myself starting to cry. It goes nowhere, life, nowhere but where it started. The difference could be the schools, but, well, why talk about it. It must be boring to have to hear it. But who does one tell anymore? Who comes to us to listen? And they tell me on the telly that England might have a problem in the next few years. My God! What are the schools for? What's life for? What can I be certain about now? Anything at all?"

3

An American Family

When Davey Sindon was small, his mother used to put him on her lap and sing, "Davey Sindon's gone to sea, leaving his father and his sister and me." No matter how often she did it, the little boy laughed and bounced up and down, trying to get her to repeat it. By the time he was five, he couldn't remember his mother Victoria ever singing to him. As for the song, Davey wasn't even certain what it meant. "Is Daddy a sailor?" he would ask his mother earnestly.

Like his older sister Effie, Davey gave his mother great pleasure. She could be tough with them, but she never did anything that made her children question her love for them. Victoria's rule was constraint. She never left the children unattended, never surprised them with sudden changes of mood. People wondered how she did it, in light of the difficulties involved in being married to Ollie Sindon, but Victoria always said, "It's easy to be a gentle boat when the sea is roaring. If the sea roars, boat don't have to do nothing but hold on to its course." Her friends would smile. Victoria had a way with words. She had a way of making the hard times seem easy, and survival, during its most precarious moments, seem effortless. She also had that special capacity of keeping people from asking her pointed questions. All one had to do was walk past the Sindon house when Ollie was going through what Victoria called his "complaining lessons," and one knew her life tottered on the point of disaster.

The problem wasn't Ollie Sindon's mercurial temperament, his fiery responses to everything from politics to changes in the weather. The problem was his being out of work; the moroseness, anger, and sickness caused by his being turned down by employers, from being lied to, from having his few little hopes shattered. "They're bombing me out," he'd roar, if he wasn't weak from drink-

15

ing. "Bombing me out with their promises and their bull shitting. I had it with those folks a long, long time ago. They hate Niggers 'til it just about kills them to have to look at us. Give us a job? Why, they'd just as soon give what little they got to an *animal* 'fore they'd give us a look. Go in there with them white faces staring at me. Oh-oh, here comes another Nigger wanting to be lazy on another job. Close the door on him 'fore he gets in too far so's we can't throw him out. You got a family, Nigger? Holy shit, here's another family man out on the street. Hey, but what the hell, Niggers don't give no shit for their families. His old lady's probably doing it with some son of a bitch right now, so what's this guy care. *Do* you care, Nigger? You Goddamn right I care, 'cause I ain't working. You hear me? If I ain't working I ain't living. You hear me, man? I'm not living no more 'til you give me a job!''

Victoria would stare at him, and without raising her voice she would warn him: "You don't talk that way with me or I take these children and I leave. I am just as upset about your not working as you are, but I will not have everybody's life being spoiled by your problems. We live on what we have, what we'll get. But don't you go playing those plays of yours. I will not be your audience any more." Then she would leave before he had a chance to speak, and by his own admission, he would be relieved that she had silenced him, for his complaining hurt him almost as much as his not working. Besides, jobs had turned up in the past, they would turn up in the future. "Just let the future come quick," he would whisper, following Victoria into the single bedroom in the apartment where the children slept. What a feeling to look down at the two of them asleep, breathing so slowly, the two of them so unaware of his problems and the miserable times they might be facing.

Ollie Sindon wanted to share his agony at being unemployed with his children, despite their being too young to understand what it meant. He wanted them to say, "Daddy, you got the rawest deal any man on this earth ever got. But you'll see, if things don't turn out better, *we're* going to make it better for you. We're going to stay by you no matter what, even if it means we'll *never* get married or move away. But no matter what happens, we'll never see you as a failure. It's the country that's at fault, not you!'' Ollie Sindon wanted so much to be happy. He saw his life as complicated, but he never gave up the idea that he could be satisfied. He was willing to settle for little, the only requirement was steady work until he was sixty-five. He dreamed of the days he would be too old to work and could say to his son, "Well sir, Davey, the load's all yours. From now on, *you* look after this family." The day dreams were plentiful, all of them with happy endings, but each one based on the idea of a man working forty hours a week and bringing home a paycheck for his wife and children.

Victoria Sindon was the only one who knew of Ollie's fantasies. She teased him about them when she was certain his mood was strong enough to take her chiding: "For someone who spends as much time dreaming as you do, your dreams don't make us too rich, do they? If I was dreaming, I'd put us in a big house somewhere, but all you see is working steady forty hours a week.''

"That's all I see," he'd answer quietly.

"Maybe that's all any of us have the right to see. Well, maybe someday you should dream about working forty-*five* hours a week. Then we'd have a little bit of extra.''

"If I start dreaming big," Ollie would say, starting to laugh, "I'm going to dream about working steady *twenty* hours a week and still end up better than what I got right now.''

"Bet you would, too.''

"You *know* I would. Then I'd add that I could see my boy working even less and getting even more. No. Let him work as long as I did, only let him come out of it a whole *helluva* lot better than I did.''

Ollie Sindon's dreams never came true. His periods of unemployment were frequent. Never a skilled laborer, no one could work harder. He quit only when the job was done, even if it meant coming home a few hours late. Victoria never liked to add to his burdens, but when he was working regularly, she wouldn't hesitate to ask about his long hours. "No one's asking you to work more than eight hours a day. You aren't that young that you can go on like a boy.''

Ollie loved to hear her talk this way. He loved the feeling of being exhausted from a hard day of work, knowing that no one in the world could tell him he hadn't put in one amazing day. "I got pride," he'd say. "I may not love what I'm doing, but I'm working, and working is the act we're put on earth to do.''

"Glad you told me," she'd wink at him, "'cause a person like myself's always happy to know why we *were* put on the earth. Now that I know it's because we get a chance to dig ditches for some rich white man, all of us can sleep better tonight.''

"Don't you fool yourself, Victoria. Everyone gets the most gratification out of his work he can. Doctor gets his kind of gratification, butcher gets his kind, even an old woman like you gets her kind. Some folks use their heads, some folks use their hands, but it don't make no difference 'cause the world needs all of us to be doing our work. There is no world without people working. I'm digging holes for telephone poles. Wouldn't exactly call it the greatest job in the world, but if I don't do it I don't stay alive.''

Victoria was happy when Ollie worked. Her children too, seemed healthier. And it was good knowing there was a little money to buy those special treats the family liked. No one in the world loved steak like Ollie Sindon. It was there when he worked; it was never mentioned when he didn't.

By the time he was eleven, Davey Sindon knew all about his father's difficulties in finding jobs. He knew it was bad luck to say anything about a job his father might get. He also knew better than to ask where his father had gone on a particular day. Maybe Ollie had worked, maybe he hadn't, but one waited to see what he would say. Most days no one had to ask; it was evident he had not worked. His eyes and posture told everything. He might ask Davey if he wanted to throw a ball around. Davey would grab their mitts and be downstairs on the street in seconds. Ollie would follow minutes later, wearing his suit jacket, and they would throw the ball back and forth, Ollie's mind a million miles away. When Ollie was working, there was real excitement in the game, and Ollie would do a play-by-play description of their game.

"There's a ground ball in the hole," he'd shout out, rolling the beaten up old ball down the sidewalk. "Sindon over to his right, makes a great pick up and throws him out. What a play!"

"Do it again," Davey would order.

"Ground ball to Sindon. He hasn't much time, Morgan can fly, but he throws him out. Get down lower, David. What, you afraid the ball's going to hit you in the face?" Davey had to admit he worried about the ball skipping off the concrete and hitting him squarely in the mouth. "Hey listen," Ollie would say, "you want to be a major leaguer, you got to take the chances. It's just another job. Man digs holes there's the danger he could fall in one of them. Man digs for coal, there's a chance he can get caught in the collapse. You go for a grounder, someone leaves a little bitty stone out there, that ball's going to pop up right over your head. Got to have fast hands, fast hands."

"You play ball, Ollie, when you were a kid?" Davey would ask.

"Did I play ball when I was a kid?" Ollie would shout back in disbelief. Victoria would be watching from the window, barely able to hear them, and making certain little Effie didn't fall off the ledge. Ollie's deep voice rushed in through the window like thick smoke. "Who do you think taught Billy George Blatter everything he knows about baseball?"

"Billy George *who*?" would come Davey's little voice.

"You don't know Billy George Blatter?" Ollie would say with exaggerated incredulity.

"No. Who's Billy George whatever his name is?"

"Victoria," Ollie would shout up to his wife. "This boy of yours doesn't know who Billy George Blatter is."

"Then suppose you just tell my son who he is."

"Tell him yourself," he'd shout, laughing to the point where his mitt would fall off and he would drop the ball, which only irritated Davey that much more.

"How the hell should I know? Anyway, hurry up because the steak's almost ready."

"Steak!" Davey would scream, dashing upstairs and leaving Ollie to carry up the mitts and ball. At dinner, Ollie would tell Davey that Billy George Blatter was a boy who went to church with him when he was little. Truthfully, he couldn't figure out why the name had come in to his mind, except that Billy Blatter was the worst athlete in the neighborhood, maybe the worst in the state. Ollie even remembered hearing the boy's father say that Billy George was so bad at sports, he must have had white blood in him. The thought made Ollie Sindon laugh out loud.

His father's enjoyment with such foolish stories irritated Davey. "We ought to have steak every night," he would say.

The remark quieted everyone.

No one knew exactly what had happened to Ollie Sindon. Merely remembering the event was difficult enough. It was a Wednesday morning, a Wednesday morning when he was out of work. He awoke and found he couldn't get out of bed. Victoria told him to quit joking, but he insisted he couldn't move his left leg. He had lost all sensation in it. Victoria was terrified. A police ambulance arrived and two attendants carried Ollie down the stairs. After several weeks, he recovered most of the feeling in the leg, although a small limp remained. While he tried to hide this slight handicap from potential employers, the few job possibilities he had accumulated grew even thinner.

The minor stroke Ollie Sindon had suffered occurred when Davey was thirteen. Victoria took on odd jobs—sewing, house cleaning, laundering—when she could find them. She disliked being away from her husband, who had grown depressed after his illness. The little bit of energy he always had been able to draw upon during the weeks of unemployment had vanished. He threatened suicide, went several days without speaking to anyone, and demanded to be fed when he knew there was no food in the house. When Victoria offered to go shopping for him he would yell at her for leaving him alone. What if he needed her suddenly? What if he fell, or suffered another stroke?

"Get someone else to go shopping for you and arrange your life to shop when Effie's here. And how come Davey isn't home at night? Just 'cause I'm not working don't mean he's supposed to be playing around all the time. What do you tell him? His father's a cripple? That his father's a bum? That why he's not here? What is it with these kids that they get so damn disrespectful? Who they think they are, anyway, acting like they're superior to everyone, wanting only this kind of food or wearing only that kind of clothes? I'd like to tell them about what *real* hard living's all about. I'd like to see them do a whole lot better what with the conditions I had facing me. Big time, that's all they want. Hell, I'll bet they sit around talking about me. 'My father don't work no more 'cause he's got a bum leg that keeps him home. 'Course even if he didn't have it he wouldn't work anyway 'cause he always had trouble. Probably didn't want to work neither. Never saw a man so lazy. Hell, he didn't even have time to play ball with me when he wasn't working. Told my mother, you're not supposed to work, then he didn't work himself. So what'd he expect, *us* to work? Laziest Nigger in the city, my father. Wasn't even a good ball player.' "VICTORIA! Where the hell are you?"

"I'm here," Victoria would scream back at him. "I am goddamn sick myself with all your complaining. You've complained about one thing or another from the day practically we got married. Now what the hell is it now? You want to eat, I told you I'd go to the store. You want to talk, we'll sit here and talk. But if it's the feel-sorry-for-the-poor-old-man bit, I have had it up to here. You want to complain about how you're the only person in the world who's got problems, you go right ahead, but I ain't listening to it, and I'll be damned if I'm ready to tell my son he has to sit here at night with his father and listen to all the garbage that flies out of your mouth!''

Ollie lisened to his wife when she spoke to him. He felt increasingly sorry for himself. He fought her, but he listened to her because, like her, he blamed himself for his troubles. Still, he fought her:

"You don't want to hear me talking, that's fine. Why don't you just take all your junk and get out of here. Take the children, empty out the kitchen, take all your friends for all I care. I'd be better off without them floating in here all the time asking me about this job or that job, or saying it don't look to me like you got any problem with your leg. Take 'em all. Or maybe you'd like *me* to leave. Why don't you go down to the five-and-dime and buy me a track suit and I'll *run* out of here. Give all of you the big laugh you want out of me. What the hell, you laugh at me behind my back, might as well do it in front of me. I sure would love to know just what it is you tell that boy about me.

"Well, son, your father's a big bust. Just another one of those dumb Niggers that didn't spend enough time in school so here he is a big failure. He tried. Even thought he'd be able to make it, but it didn't work out. Tell you, son, there's only one thing a man's supposed to do, and that's work. If he don't work, well, he just ain't a man. So you see, son, your old man ain't a man at all. He's just a dumb old NIGGER!''

"Shut up," Victoria would cry out. "Shut up or I *will* leave."

"Go on. Who the hell needs you around here anyway—all you do is mother people. Hell, you been mothering me like I was the boy's brother instead of his father."

"You act like you were his *baby* brother 'stead of his father. 'Bout time you started acting like his father."

"'Bout time you shut your face up."

"I don't see where just because you ain't working don't mean you can't take a fatherly interest in him."

"A fatherly interest in him," he would mock her. "You know something, Victoria, you're beginning to sound like some of those high class white folks you been working for. Maybe that's what you want, too, since you *are* the man of the family. Ain't that it?"

"What you want to eat?"

"I'm asking you a question," he would scream at her.

"What do you want me to say?"

''I want you to say that because I don't work I'm only his father by title. I carry the title, like I carry a card saying I got a right to work. Neither of them does no good. I'm a shit ass father and you know it. But I ain't making excuses to nobody. Don't care what happens to either of them, 'cause *I* come first, man. *I'm* the one. I don't have a job, there ain't no work in this country, bad leg or not, then I don't mess around with no children. That's *your* job. Don't give a damn about them. Don't need to see them, don't need to talk to them. Boy wants to talk with some man, let him find somebody at his school. Better yet, let him go find one of those bullshit Nigger ministers. You want real men with real jobs, men working their asses off for the community just for the love of God, then that's who he can go talk to. He can go in the church with all those other guys running around in there. 'Hey man, what you do?' 'I work for God, man.' 'Oh yeah? What you do for God, man?' 'I light candles and keep people from sinning.' 'Yeah, that right, man?' 'Yeah. Get money for it, too, telling all the little children with fathers who don't work what to do.' 'Yeah, what you tell 'em to do?' 'I tell 'em how they got to have *compassion* for their poor old stumbling fathers. Poor old man sitting up there in his ridiculous little house watching the walls and waiting to die. Got to *advise* all those little children so's they see the light of God.' 'Hey, man, that's one helluva job you got there working for the church. I talk to those children myself, man.' 'Yeah? Ones with the unemployed fathers?' 'Sure, man. I talk to 'em just like you do.' 'That a fact? And what do *you* tell 'em?' 'I tell 'em if you're old enough to see your old man ain't working, and you're old enough to understand that when he don't work it means he ain't bringing home a fuckin' dime, then you're old enough to get away from that man as soon as you can 'cause he *ain't* no man. He *ain't* no father. He's nothing, man. And the sooner you forget the sight of him, the better off you're going to be. Don't hang around him if he ain't working. Man will just bring you down with him.' "

Victoria would close the door to the apartment and start down the stairs quietly. She would be weeping. Then Ollie's big voice would bellow from the living room. "Victoria, Victoria, you get back in here at once. You come back in this house in one minute or I won't be here when you get back. You can just say goodbye right now."

Victoria would go buy strawberry ice cream for him, even though the doctor said Ollie would do better without starchy foods.

No matter how hard she tried, Victoria Sindon never convinced her husband that being out of work did not reflect on him as a man or father. But there was no assuring him. A job possibility would arise and his spirits lifted, but Victoria could see that he was scared now from the uncertainty and the months of inactivity. There were days when the little bit of hope she wanted to hold on to seemed real enough, but no jobs ever lasted, and Ollie wasn't getting any younger. Indeed, he seemed to be aging more quickly than anyone she knew, with the exception of her son.

At fourteen, Davey Sindon was a strong young man, quiet, and filled with anger. He rarely let even his closest friends know what he was thinking and feeling. His father had lost touch with him, and his mother, he insisted, hadn't the slightest notion of who he was. A complex person with many talents, he dreamed of becoming many things. But in conversations that dwelled on his life, his father's unemployment inevitably played a significant role. It was like a fire that never went out. He himself could never say precisely what angered him: Was it widespread unemployment, or the mere fact that his father spent so much time out of work? He might start a tirade against America, its racism and poverty, but soon he was raging against his father, calling him weak and a quitter. He labeled his father the nice little Nigger in the company of white folks. The odds, he would always say, were so stacked against families like his, the only way to lead one's life was to take the attitude that you had everything to win and nothing to lose, except the respect of a few people, like perhaps your own father.

Davey's manner troubled his mother and infuriated his father. "They're all fancy big shots," Ollie would growl when Davey went out on a Friday night. "Son of a bitch child looks down his nose at me, and there he is strutting around as if he were the goddamn tax collector. If he disapproves of me so much, let him get his own goddamn home. If he can do so much better without me, let's see him try. While he's at it, he can go show this great big world he thinks he's discovering to his sister. Then *she* can be a phoney big shot too. Where'd he get those clothes?"

Victoria held the same fears as her husband about where her son went and what he did. Her problem was to get Ollie to turn his attention from his own concerns to those of his son. Ollie himself said that his salvation lay in making certain his children wouldn't share the fate he had known, but something always kept him from putting his own problems aside long enough to attend to his children. No matter now intensely he resolved to devote himself to Davey, his bitterness at being sickly and out of work kept him from carrying out his intentions.

"You know where that boy's going to end up, Victoria?" Ollie would mutter.

"I know exactly where he's going to end up. He's going to end up in jail. Won't be long now."

"Way you say it, makes it sound like that's what you want."

Victoria wouldn't bother to respond.

The thought that he might end up in jail also had crossed Davey Sindon's mind: "Could happen, man," he would say. "Steady work though, in jail, ain't it? I mean, you don't even have to go looking for it, or have some Mr. Nobody with a big stomach interview you or nothing. You walk in there and the cat says 'your job's working in the carpentry shop.' They even pay you to work. Ain't much, but what the hell, working for peanuts is better than not working. You don't believe me, you just ask my old man. Man, has this country screwed *that* guy up. Down on his knees, I'll bet, more times than he'd ever admit begging for people to give him a job. So what the hell if I am in jail. They give me the work, I'll blow out my time there.

"'Course my old man, he'd be angry. Love to see that man's face when the cat comes and tell him, 'We got your boy locked up for ripping off a bank.' 'Son of a bitch kid,' he'd yell at my mother. 'Told you he was no good. Yeah, but tell me, Copper, how much the boy rip that bank off for? Couple thousand maybe?' Couple thousand, man? Shit. I may go into prison somewhere, if they catch me. But if I go I ain't going for no two thousand dollars, baby. I go in for the kill. Six figures right up front man, or I don't even *talk* about the job. You see my old man starting to smile. Is that a fact? Old Davey boy ripped 'em off for six figures? Son of a bitch kid didn't do so bad at that, even if he is in prison. Hell, time will come when they got to let him out. 'Say, tell me, Copper, they find out maybe he left a little money for his poor old mom and dad? Ain't worked in twenty years, man. Bet he left a little something outside for me.' 'Hell, he did, old man. Told me to tell you you played the good Nigger too long man. You could have been in on anything you wanted.' Sitting in that chair of his, bitching all the time 'bout this and that to my mother, my *mother*, man, like she was the governor or something.

"You get a load of that guy, man, begging in the streets so's he got the whole community laughing at him, and he's putting it to my mother? What the hell he think she's ever going to do for *him*. She walked blocks, man, more streets than you could count, looking for the food he told her he wanted. You imagine that, man, sending that woman 'round the city shopping in just the stores *he* wants, buying him just the certain kind of ice cream he wants, 'cause you can't get the brand in stores 'round here? Son of a bitch worked, hell, no more than a few years all together since he was married, and he's pushing her 'round like he's some king. Should have seen him too when he got sick, you know with that leg of his. Doctor told my mother he was fine. He went around acting like they took his leg off. Made everybody treat him special like he was somebody famous. He's nothing, man. He can't stand to face it, but he's nothing. You want to bullshit guys at the poolhall, let 'em think you ain't drawing welfare? That's okay, man. Nobody says you got to advertise your losses, you know what I mean. But he was acting like he was doing all right in his own home. Front of me and my mother and my sister. Who's he think he's kidding?

"And that's another thing. All this time he ain't working, all he's thinking about is me. Half the time I think he's trying to figure out ways I won't end up like him. But the other half, man, I really think the son of a bitch was plotting how to have me end up in the same shit pile as him. I think it'd kill him to see me successful when he failed so bad. There ain't no one talked so bad as he did. But don't think once he's paid any attention to my sister. I can't even remember him asking her what's she doing, like at school. And that kid is smart, man. She reads out loud to my mother sometimes at night. I tell her to shut up 'cause I'm trying to sleep, but I'm only pretending 'cause I love to hear her read. My mother gets her all these adult books and she goes through them, zip zap zip. She remembers 'em too. I do too when I hear her reading them out loud. But you think my old man has once said, hey, you know what Effie, you're the best reader in this city. I'm proud of you, Effie. I love you, Effie. Fuck you, Effie. Don't say a word to her. Man's got no job so he thinks he's got the right to order us around. Nobody's told him you got to earn your place in the house. You don't just get it for free.

"Other thing he thinks about is how soon it's going to be 'fore I end up in the slammer. Shit, I got a mind to walk in on him one day and say, 'Listen here, I'm going to take a big load off your mind. I'm going to be in jail in less than a year, so now all you got to worry about is feeling sorry for yourself. But don't trouble yourself none, 'cause it wouldn't look right, your getting off your sweet ass trying to find a job somewhere so's your old lady might have a couple of nice days on the earth before she croaks. And while I'm in jail, why the hell don't you introduce yourself to the little skinny girl who lives in the same apartment as you. You named her after your own mother so you must have been interested in her once. 'Stead of sitting there trying to convince everybody you can't walk and that's why you don't go looking for a job, have her read out loud to you. Shit, man, I'm not so sure my old man even knows how to read himself. Guess he must, I see him with the newspaper every day, Don't do him a helluva lot of good though, does it? Maybe he don't know they print jobs available in it. Probably all he's doing is choking himself to death on the comics.

"I don't know, sometimes I feel sorry for the guy. Tell myself, hey, the world is tough, 'specially if you're black. Lots of folks out of work. Nobody cares all that much about how many folks don't have jobs when it's just black folks. People going around mumbling, uppity Niggers won't work for twenty cents an hour no more. Then all of a sudden, like, all these white dudes, they start losing their jobs too, high paying guys too, lots of 'em. Then that's *all* you hear about, unemployment, unemployment. Ten years ago nobody said a word. Now everybody's bitching and moaning. Who was looking out for my old man ten years ago? Nobody, man. They were out there on the streets looking for the cheapest labor they could find. Hell, they knew they could buy men like my father cheap, and man did they ever give 'em the shittiest jobs. They had my father standing waist high in shit, digging, and the son of a bitch came home proud of his work, telling my mother he did a good day's work. They paid him shit, man, for working in shit, and the man felt proud. I can't believe it, man. He used to come home, he'd be smelly like you couldn't imagine. Me and my sister couldn't stand how much he smelled. We had to get out of the house, man. My father and mother pretended to be angry with us for walking out like that, but you could see they were only pretending. Everybody was happy then 'cause the man had work. I was happy too. I mean, I wasn't old enough to be ashamed of what he did for a living. What's your old man do, David? My old man stands ass high in shit and shovels it around, but he's happy 'cause he's got a steady job. Little kids ain't ashamed of their fathers. They don't know what being out of work is all about.

"But all that's different now, man. He never works. I ain't got a reason in the world why I should stay around the house. I might have thought he was pretty cute when I was small, but I don't see nothing cute about him now. It's my job to make sure my mother and Effie are going to be all right, 'cause he sure gave up on that job a long, long time ago. He'll push my mother around, man, about the slightest thing that bothers him. 'Hey, Victoria, how come my shirts ain't clean? Hey, Victoria, how come your son's always getting into trouble?' But she takes it. Maybe there's something wrong with her too, to take all his pushing her around. Hell, if I was her I'd tell him, 'Hey, lookit here, man. You work for a living, get up off your ass one second of the day and I'll *think* about obeying some of your orders. But if you just sit there looking so goddamn mad at the world, I wouldn't go across this room to open the goddamn window for you.' She don't tell him nothing though, man. It's almost like he's got some special right to be out of work. It's like he's always telling her, lots of guys like him out of work. You can't argue with the man. Black folks are getting killed without a job. They'll take a black man's job from him ten times faster than a white man's job. You got a bunch of cats working on some big construction job and the word comes down to cut off some men, who you think they're going to cut first? They'll cut every black man off that job unless the dude is so well trained they can't get along without him. But there ain't a lot of specialized cats 'cause they don't train 'em until they've trained all the white guys they can find. Shit, jobs being what they are, you can be damn sure that cat's going to turn his back on his own brothers if he can save his job.

"So who's my father got helping *him* out in the world, man? There ain't nobody, unless it's somebody watching him figuring out how he's going to take my old man's job, if he ever gets one. Guy don't stand a chance. He's got a one in million chance, man, just to earn a living. You imagine how that makes him feel? Man has to pull his body out of the bed every morning knowing he's got a one in a million chance to make his goddamn living. It's no wonder he got sick like he did. This thing breaks your spirit; there's nothing left of the guy. When I was small, you know, and he was working, that man was fun to have around. Man used to play ball with me, cat was a stitch. He'd make it fun for me, 'cause it sure couldn't have been too much fun for him. Hell, I couldn't catch the damn thing and half the time I had him running in the street or down some cellar stairs. But he was a jive, man. Folks used to stand around and watch him. He knew everybody, man. After work, all the men would come down to watch my old man play ball, and all these little kids wanted to play with us. He knew I didn't want to play with 'em. He knew what I was thinking even without me saying a word. He'd tell 'em, this scene's just with me and my son. This here's our special after work baseball game. Man, I felt fantastic. I'd think, son of a bitch, man has to be the greatest father alive.

"Hey, but you grow up, you learn what's happening in the world. You see your father sitting home all the time, bitching 'bout that, moaning 'bout that, and no matter what he says about how black folks got it tough, I see him not working. Words are one thing, but what he does or doesn't do, that's a whole other thing.

And the dude ain't working. Just picking on my old lady, which means he's probably knocking hell out of her when me and Effie ain't there. But she don't say much. I used to think to myself, I'm going out to make money. I'll give 'em both all my money. You see me, ten years old looking for a job? Get me fifty, sixty thou' a year and give it to my folks. Little kids and all their dreams, huh?

"I didn't know what to do with either one of my folks when it got bad. I said to myself, I'm either going to run away, or I swear to God I'm going to kill 'em both 'cause they're both crazy. I'm watching my mother, this is like two years ago, and she's not well. But I don't say nothing. What am I going to do about it anyway? I was waiting for my old man to do something, but he didn't move up off his ass far as I could tell. So one day I come home from school and I got to take a piss something terrible, man. So I run upstairs thinking for sure I'm going to do it in my pants and I like fly into the toilet, and there's my mother sitting there crying. She's surprised to see me, but the tears are all *over* her face. I didn't have to piss no more. I mean, you see your mother and she's all by herself and she's crying . . . So I ask her 'What's wrong?' and she keeps saying, 'Nothing's wrong, nothing's wrong.' 'But you're crying.' 'That ain't nothing,' she says. 'I don't know why I was crying. Something in my eye.' You got something in your eye you ain't sitting in the bathroom looking like she looked. My father was sitting in the living room like he always did, he didn't even know she was in there, 'cause I went in there and asked him. He called her, you know, 'You crying, Victoria?' and she comes out and says 'No.' She don't have to tell me not to tell him no more. I can see plain as hell she don't want him to know nothing about nothing.

"Then nothing happens for a while. My mother's going 'round acting like everything's fine. Then about a month later I heard my aunt talking to my mother's best friend. They were outside on the sidewalk and I hid behind the door. My aunt is talking and she's telling Morane how my mother's sick and what the doctors have to do, which is to go, like, once a week and get an x-ray. I can't figure out what they're talking about 'cause I thought x-ray was like when you broke something. But this was something different. Anyway, I figured some of it out and Morane told me the rest later. My mother had cancer, maybe she still has it, and she was afraid to say nothing about it to my father 'cause she didn't want to bother him about it 'cause he was too upset about his own life to hear any *more* bad news. You believe that woman acting like that? Shit, man, I get cancer and wonder if I'm going to die any minute, I'd go crying to anybody I could find, and the first person I'd cry to is my husband. He tell me not to moan 'cause he's got worse problems, I tell him to get the fuck out of this house and don't ever come back!

"That woman hid that she was sick from him. He didn't know 'til after she was done going for those treatments. Then she had to keep going back to see if she was well. They can burn you up but good and it still grows back. I learned all this from one of my teachers. She said, you worried by all this, David? I said no, what's to be worried about? She's only got it in one part of her body. I didn't even know where she had it. When I found out I almost threw up. I mean, I never thought too much about how women are put together, then this teacher tells me how they do it and I imagined my mother lying there on this table and them putting this machine over her, man, and it doing whatever it does, and all I could think about was her sitting in that bathroom and not telling my father 'cause she was worried about *him* all the time. About *him*, 'cause he was always so down about not working. Shit, I'd have killed the man for acting like that with her being sick. Never got her flowers or nothing, or helped her in the house. The both of them were just walking around pretending nothing was wrong. I couldn't believe it, man, and Effie didn't know nothing about none of it. Didn't even know my mother was sick, and I didn't know if she was better from all the treatment. Even my mother didn't know if Morane knew about what was going on, and she for sure didn't know what *I* knew. When I told my teacher, you know, not to say nothing to my folks, she goes, 'I didn't even know your father was alive. You never say nothing about him.' It was true too, 'cause most of the time at school I pretended like he was dead 'cause I never wanted no one asking about him.

''But the thing was, my dad was upset by everything going on. He got scared about my mother same as I did. Then he got feeling sorry 'cause he'd been such a bad husband to her. That's all he could say for months. He was like a little kid. I didn't know whether to feel sorry for the guy 'cause he had no job and his wife might be dying, or pissed off 'cause he was acting like a baby. You could love him or hate him practically in the same minute. Hell, I got so frustrated from seeing him acting like he did, I decided I'm getting out of that house as much as I can. I know my father real well, and I know what he was thinking. He was thinking, Dear Lord, let me find a job with my wife sick. I'll do *anything* but I need a job *now*. But he couldn't get nothing, man. So between him not working and my mother lying on that table with that x-ray machine burning her insides out, where a woman has her baby, you know, you can imagine how we were doing.

''Effie, though, she was doing fine. She'd come home and read and help my mother. You couldn't tell by looking at her she knew anything different from before. So one day I took her outside and I said to her, 'Effie, you got any idea what's going on in our house?' 'You mean Dad not working?' she goes. 'I say, that ain't new.' 'You mean about Mom and the x-ray treatments?' 'You know where she's getting them?' 'At the hospital,' she goes. 'Not in the hospital. Where in her body, you know, where they're working on her?' 'Yeah.' She knew. 'They're working on her uterus,' she said. 'On her *what*?' 'Don't worry about it none,' she goes, 'you ain't got one so you ain't going to get sick there.' And all that time I was walking 'round trying to make sure my kid sister doesn't know what's happening. So I asked her, 'How come you know so much?' So she says, ''Cause I talked to the same teacher you did. She even gave me a book to read.' Effie's going to be all right, even though she is the daughter of a sick old mother and a father who's barely staying alive.

"Then there's me. I got the same parents and look at me. Kind of sad, I'd say, way I'm turning out. I'm sure it makes my parents sad too. I don't know what Effie thinks. She can't think much of me. Most of the time now I don't know whether to blame people for what's happening or just forget them or what. Talking with my old man doesn't help, 'cause no matter how good he sounds when he's talking, I just can't get up the respect for the guy. Like, when he talks to me about being a man, it'd be a whole lot better if someone else was talking 'cause he ain't much of a man himself. I mean, I'm sitting there, and the man's telling me about working and making steady money and taking vacations, which is something we never did once in our life. I don't blame him for nothing, but what's he talking about living in the middle class scene for when he ain't worked, like, for years? There ain't nothing he's done that makes him so much of a man he can talk like that to me. Hell, it ain't nothing to be a father; it's the woman does all the work. My old man could have done a lot more than he did too, 'cause he didn't have nothing else to do with himself. Just like me now. We both got all the time in the world on our hands. Neither one of us no better than the other."

David Sindon was fifteen years old when he knifed Jared Alexander in a street fight. Both boys had been drinking. Nobody knew what started the fight. David had cajoled a woman into buying liquor for a group of boys, then suddenly he and Jared were fighting. Jared produced a long knife, David broke a bottle and foolishly threw it at Jared, leaving himself without a weapon. But Peter Mixley threw him his knife and the boys wrestled around and fell over one another. Finally, a gurgling painful sob came from Jared, and he was lying doubled up in the street, a knife stuck in his abdomen. Blood was everywhere and the boys were terrified. At first, David thought of leaving Jared there, but Peter insisted they had to call the police. David argued with him, but another boy already had run off to get help.

David Sindon was charged with manslaughter and put in jail to await trial. His parents were sickened by the news. They visited him every day, nervous and confused by the long wait before his trial. A court-appointed lawyer met with David three times in four months.

Victoria Sindon had not responded well to the x-ray treatment and underwent surgery. The cancer had spread to her bowel, a section of which was removed. Her son cried when he heard the news of the operation. Effie came to the prison but David refused to see her. She was too good and too smart, he said, to get messed up by his troubles. She offered to read to him but he refused this too, even though he loved listening to her. Ignoring his request, she brought him magazines. She had landed a job with a neighborhood store and spent her money on little gifts for him and Victoria who was recuperating at home. Amazingly, Effie's school work never faultered, despite the family's burdens falling on her shoulders. "Effie's going to make it," Ollie said. "With her brother and her mother and me and every other problem in the world she has to face, the girl's still going to make it.''

Friends rallied around the Sindons. Everyday someone else was in the apartment, preparing food, cleaning up, attending to Victoria and allowing Effie time to do her school assignments. David's friends washed windows and floors and went on errands for the Sindons. Gradually Victoria seemed to be recovering, but Ollie had become quiet and depressed. No one could convince him that what he called his collapse as a man hadn't brought down his entire family. He made arrangements to visit his son every day. When David rejected him, he sat in the jail's waiting room, his eyes fixed on the door leading to the cells. When visiting hours ended, he rose and walked to the bus stop, and began the two-hour journey home.

In the year following David's trouble, Ollie Sindon lost fifty pounds. Whereas once he had an enormous appetite, he now missed meals. He ate better on the evenings when his son met with him, but even these occasions didn't lift his spirit. He blamed himself for everything; this was his punishment.

"Going to starve myself," he said, "'til I find out about my son. It ain't going to be good with him no matter how it comes out, but it don't make no difference to the way I feel about myself. You take any human tragedy, and you'll find right off the person who's to take the blame for it. You may not be able to put your finger on him, but he's there. I can go the rest of my life saying, bad economic times, that's why there weren't jobs. I can say, black folks always have it the worst. But some black men found work. Even if they have 20 percent unemployed, they still have 80 percent employed, and a lot of that 80 percent is black, ain't they? So lots of men living right in this community may be in the same boat I am, but most of 'em ain't. There *is* someone to blame, and you don't need the police to find him.

"My life has been wasted, and wasteful. Never was much as a kid, ain't much more as a man. I have a wife who wouldn't be as bad if I was working. Got a kid in jail who for sure wouldn't be there if I was working. I got Effie, bless her. Maybe I go on just for her, or maybe for all of 'em, I don't even know. I could quit. You got lots of folks in this country quitting where I'm going on, you know. Guys blowing their brains out when they lose their jobs. Rich ones, too. Folks used to having everything they want and suddenly they got a whole new life. They see where it's at. You got lots of reasons to call it quits. Saddest thing to me is I don't even know how to go about thinking about all this. I never did much at school, quit going to church a long time ago. When I do go I don't learn anything from it. I don't even know what I'm supposed to know about living and dying. Way it looks to me now is the whole point of living is dying. 'Cept I know there's one helluva lot more to living than that. I didn't think much of dying when I was working regular. Just took what come each day and let it go. Times got tough, things would just work themselves out, I'd say. Now I ain't got anything else *to* think about.

''Whole thing's a goddamn war. That enemy out there is beating the shit out of me, man, and I'm not up to taking it much longer, which is probably a lie, 'cause I been taking it this long I might just go on and on taking it. Man like me wants to yell out, it's somebody else's fault. But it's my fault. I could have done it so it would have come out better. But now, I don't even know how to go about thinking this thing through. My boy don't want to talk to me, my wife's been sick, my daughter could go at any time, and I'm walking around wishing my mother was still on the earth so she could fix everything. Now is that the way a man goes through his life, wishing his mamma were here to take care of him? That's a beaten man talking. That's no winner coming at you. I got so much pain now; pain inside—pain not a doctor in the world could fix. Take one pain away and I'd come up with a hundred more to take its place.

''Holy Jesus, give me a break, will you. Ain't it been long enough? You want to punish me, okay, but get it the hell over with already. What I need to take more pain for? I'll tell you why He gives me all that pain too. Because He knows I can take it. He knows I ain't about to jump out of no window or stick no gun down my throat. He's got an easy victim with me. Tells all His angels, 'Lookit down there at old man Sindon. Got a boy in jail, got a wife going to go back to the hospital one of these days, that's the guy you want to give your pain to. Man hasn't worked all these years, so he's got nothing to do with his time but take all your pain. So give it to him. I know that man down there, he'll take it, has no choice but to take it. We're going to give him the job he's been looking for all these years. We're going to give him the job of taking all this pain. You hear us, Ollie, we got a full time job for you. You're going to be working day and night, seven days a week being a pain hauler. Don't make no money hauling pain, but it'll keep you out of trouble. Keep you from eating like you should and sleeping like you should. Just relax now, man, 'cause we got mountains of the stuff for you to haul, and you got the rest of your life to do it. What the hell, man, you ought to be in good shape for it too. You ain't been doing nothing to tire yourself out for the last ten years. You deserve it, man. This job is *marked* for you. You're the only man who can do it, you pain hauler you!' ''

4

Hey, Harrington,
There's a Kid on the Phone
Says He's Your Son

In the beginning, it was true that Eddie Harrington ran out of the house when his father disappeared on his binges and sat by himself or took long walks. In the beginning, he could not have been further from the boys in the neighborhood who seemed to find trouble no matter where they went, or what plans they made. He wanted no part of anybody. When he thought he saw people he knew he would duck into an alley or bolt across the empty lot near the project on Tyler Street. And he would talk to himself.

"I'd tell myself, 'Okay, man. Get hold of yourself, don't let yourself go all the way.' Stupid things like that. I couldn't understand my dad just walking out on us. I didn't think I was blaming him, because I didn't want to blame him. He's not a bad guy or anything. I knew he had a lot of problems. I guess I was always a little afraid of him, more than a little when he'd be fired from his job—he never admitted to anyone that he was fired but he was. Sometimes he was laid off, like a lot of men around here, but sometimes he was just fired. I was always hoping he'd come and talk with me. I was the oldest boy in the family and, you know, sometimes that happens. But he'd just go. I told him lots of times I'd like to go with him where he goes, but he said I had to stay around home 'cause I had school and stuff like that. Once he said, even if I cut school or quit for good— which he didn't want me to do—I could find better things to do than go with him. Honest, that's what he told me. I never told him nothing, but I was thinking that I'll never do anything that'll amount to all that much if I stay in school or quit this minute. I'm not meant to become much of anything. Never was either, even if things in my family or at school had been different."

In time, the running away to be by himself turned into running away and being consumed with fear. It was as if he were dreading the coming of a momentous event, a calamity even. Now he would hide in the corner of the project's small playfield as the afternoons grew dark, keeping an eye out for something unusual, a sign that the calamity was about to occur. In describing this new sense of dread, he once compared himself to a guard at the airport checking people's luggage to make certain no one was carrying a bomb. From his hiding places, he studied people's faces and memorized the shapes of buildings, counting the number of windows, and estimating the lengths and widths of door frames and fire escapes.

One night, on an occasion when his father had gone away, Eddie, who was then thirteen, collected a huge pile of newspapers and placed them in a dilapidated sandbox in the project playground, not far from one of the ground-floor apartments. Then he took some papers, rolled them up, and dipped them into the gas tank of a motorcycle he found parked two blocks away behind the supermarket. He recognized the cycle as belonging to Butchie Mayo, who worked as a checker at the market. After running through the streets with the newspaper smelling of gasoline, he reached the pile of papers in the sandbox. Carefully making certain that no one saw him, he set fire to the damp newspaper and threw it on the pile. In minutes a huge fire rose up from the sandbox. Suddenly people were running into the playground from their apartments and from the street. A woman leaned out the window of her kitchen and screamed for help. The fire was quickly put out by two men and the people who gathered near the sandbox returned to their homes wondering how it could have started. Eddie Harrington was never caught.

He repeated the action two weeks later. This time he could not find one reason for his behavior. His father was still out of work but had been showing up at home now and again. Eddie's school work was not that bad. There just seemed to be something pushing him to start a fire.

"I can't explain it," he would say later. "Sometimes things just come into my head, so I have to do them. Like, I'll be sitting on my bed, you know, and I won't be thinking anything special, but then suddenly I'm slamming my fist into the wall, really hurt it too. Only I don't even know that I'm doing it. And like, when I do it, when my hand hits the wall, that's like the first time I think about it. Maybe there's another me inside the one everybody sees ordering me to do things. I suppose that'd be all right, except it would be nice to know that this other person, the one inside me, was ordering me to do good things too, not only bad things."

Then Eddie Harrington paused, as though he had actually caught sight of that other person inside himself.

"I think my problems are due to my parents, 'specially my father, although I hate to blame him. Maybe I'm even a little afraid to blame him. But like, when a kid like me grows up, he kind of expects his dad and mother to be certain ways. Like, first off, he expects them to be married or not married, right? Or like with my folks, if they don't have enough money to get a divorce, let them be separate with the kids sort of knowing, over here's where your mother lives and over there's where your father lives. But none of this maybe they are together and maybe they aren't because nobody can tell because one time he's here and then he's not for a couple of days—or maybe weeks—and then he's back again. I mean, they got to make up their minds where they stand, 'specially if they got a family, kids and all.

"So the next thing I think kids got a right to expect is that their father or mother got a job. In my case I think it should be my father who has a job 'cause he ain't separated from us. They don't have a divorce, so why shouldn't he have a job? Nobody ever asks him to do anything around the house, so why shouldn't a kid like me and my sisters expect him to be working? Like with us, we never get the real picture of what's going on with my father. Not that it has to be our business, because if the guy doesn't want to tell us what's going on in his life, he don't have to. But when he isn't working, when you see him hanging around the house doing nothing—and I mean day after day, all the time—then he ought to explain it. 'Specially to me. I'm his son. And *he's* suppose to be training *me* for when I'm a man. I got to get a job some day. But he doesn't trust us enough to tell us anything I guess, 'cause he should be telling us what's going on.

"I don't see that much of my father. Lots of guys I know, they see their father all the time, and some of 'em, they never see 'em. But not only don't I know what he does, I don't even know where he goes. If I was little, you know, like a baby just walking or talking, I wouldn't care all that much. Like, I would know how a father is supposed to be. Hell, I wouldn't even know there *is* such a thing as a father. But now, I understand all of it. He's as good as any other guy like him. I mean, he don't have any real education, any skill for doing much. He can't just join a union. They don't take anybody. A guy has to prove he can sweat pipes or fix gutters, you know, before they can even figure out what union he's supposed to join. But like with my father, he can't do that much. He wants to, he wants to work, I know that 'cause he's told us lots of times. But where's he going to get a job? Where's he going to find anything for any amount of money? He'd take anything, man. I know he would. He doesn't talk that way to us. He couldn't. I couldn't either if I was him. But he'd take anything. A guy comes to the house tomorrow and says, 'Hey, Mr. Harrington, we got a job for you shoveling shit off the dock into the river,' he'd take it in a minute. He'd ask them, 'How much the job pay?' 'Specially if one of us was standing around listening to him. Maybe he'd say, "Well let me think about it. I don't know that a guy like me wants to shovel shit for the rest of his life.' But hell, they offer him steady work for two days a week, he'd grab it.

"My father's ashamed he's out of work. You can see it just the way he's, like, afraid to look at us. He don't even want to be seen. He's hiding from us. I'd be that way too. Like, when I don't do my work in school I hide from everybody, 'specially my teachers. I don't know what they'd say but I don't want to know.

My dad hides the same way. He's like a little boy. He tells me all the time, 'You got to be a man. Don't let people beat you or get the best of you, you know what I mean.' But he can't be that way himself. And you know why? 'Cause he's begging. He's a street beggar. That's all. He's begging for anything he can get and he don't like it. You know when you go 'round and see those run-down old guys begging in the street? I used to see them walking with my dad sometimes. He'd tell me, 'Never want to give people like that money. They had the strength they'd go out and find a job like the rest of us.' But now he's just like them, only he's got too much pride to go out there and be like them. Jesus, I just thought how that would feel, walking down the street with your friends and seeing all these beggars, all of them reaching out their hands like they'd take the money out of your pocket if you don't give it to them, and suddenly, there's your father, you know, begging for money that maybe he gave you that morning. I don't even know if I'd say hello to him. Fact I know I wouldn't. I'd be too embarrassed, just like my dad is now.

"I understand the way he is. I'd tell him if he gave us the chance. He shouldn't be ashamed. All of us know what's going on with jobs. He ain't the first guy out of work around here, and he sure won't be the last. It's going to get worse. I just wish he'd give us the chance to talk about it with him so he wouldn't have to keep going away all the time like he does, and I wouldn't have this other person in me telling me I got to do things that get me in trouble. Hell, I'm bound to end up in jail. Maybe meet my old man in there one of these days. The rate we're both heading there's a good chance of that too."

The lighting of fires lasted for several months. They stopped abruptly when Eddie Harrington was picked up by a policeman as he was about to ignite a pile of newspapers and garbage behind a bakery shop. The policeman had been watching as Eddie made his preparations. Believing that Eddie was going to rob the bakery when people rushed out to see the fire, the policeman chose to wait. In fact he saw Eddie merely standing nearby. Calling him a sick pyro, the policeman took him to the precinct station where, as Eddie describes it, six or seven officers questioned him.

"You should have seen them, they couldn't wait to get their hands on me. They acted like I was the number one most wanted crook in the country. I couldn't believe it. All these guys, I almost asked them how come they didn't have anything better to do with themselves than ask me all these stupid questions. I didn't say that, of course, 'cause mostly I was scared. Just the way they got the place set up makes it scary, and not just for kids. Like, the only things they have on the walls are posters of prisoners and crooks. Honest to God. You'd think they'd put something on the walls, make it a little nicer for them. They do that much at school, and there can't be no rooms in the world uglier than what we got in school. I mean they're terrible. And these cops, they got to *work* there all day and all night. You'd think they'd like it nicer.

"First they didn't do nothing with me. Just let me sit there. They put me in this room in the back somewhere, dragging me through the halls like they'd just arrested Al Capone or somebody. You could tell they weren't too excited by it, acting tough and laughing a lot. This guy who arrested me, he laughed all the time they were taking me to the station. Then we get there and they put me in this room and nobody says nothing. I sat there and sat there and nobody ever came in, not even by accident. I could have gone outside but I just sat there. So finally this guy comes in, a cop, and he says. 'Who the hell are you? Aren't you a little young to be sitting there like that? What the hell you do anyway, rob a nursery?' And he laughs too. So I say to him, real polite, 'Can I go?' So he says, 'How the hell should I know? I don't even know why you're here so how should I know if you can go? Who booked you?' That's what he asked me. Who booked you? Like, I wanted to say to the guy, 'What do you think I did, tell the cop who picked me up that before he arrested me he had to tell me his name?' I didn't say nothing, and this guy goes away too. So I sit there another two hours and nobody comes in. I remember it started out light outside but I could see through the window it was getting darker and darker, and I was getting hungrier and hungrier.

"So finally I go out and I'm walking through the halls of the station, honest to God. I'm free as a bird walking around looking in all the rooms. And all these cops there, they saw me, none of 'em said a thing to me. I'm walking around the halls and they're going about their business. So I ask this one guy, 'Are you supposed to question me?' He goes, 'Who are you?' So I tell my name, and he yells out, 'We got an Eddie Harrington here for some reason?' and this other cop at the desk who looked like he was drunk or something, he says, 'Nope, nobody here by that name.' So the cop says I should go back to the room where I was. I could have walked out of there any time. I didn't have to talk to any of them. I could have just walked out. I could have pretended I was one of the policeman's sons, just walking around looking for my father. Then I thought, what if I walked into some room and I really did see my father, being a prisoner, although as far as I know my dad never got into trouble with cops. I think my sister and me were the first in the family.

"Anyway, I go back in this room and wait. Then, like at nine or ten o'clock—I never did know what time it was in there—this big fat cop comes in, guy with the reddest face I ever saw with all these pimples and sores all over his nose and cheeks. He comes in there and he says, 'Okay let's have it.' So I start to tell him about the fire and he stops me. He says, 'First off, who's your father?' So I tell him. Then he says, 'What's your father do?' So I tell him, 'I don't know,' 'cause I don't, and he says I'm being fresh. So I tell him again my dad don't work. So he says, 'What is he, a crook or just out of work?' So I tell him he's out of work, like for a lot of months. So the cop says, 'Call him on the phone,' and he gives me a dime. So I tell him I don't know where he is. He'd been around the house but I was afraid to tell him what happened. Then I thought, if my father gives me shit for getting into trouble starting fires, I'll tell him *he's* the reason I do it 'cause he's never around the house even when he isn't working.

"So the cop says, 'Call your home.' And I'm sitting there thinking, how come you don't fix all those pimples you got hiding your nose. So I call home with his dime 'cause, like, I did have some money with me when they arrested me but they took everything when they brought me in there. My sister Elaine, she was the only one home. She said my father wasn't around but she had a number where maybe I could get him. So I have to ask this cop with the nose for another dime. So he says, 'What the hell you think this is, a goddam bank?' He wasn't all that bad, but he was starting to think I was going to call every number in this city on his bread. Anyway, I call this number Elaine give me and this woman answers. So she says, "Yeah, he's here, who are *you*?' So I say, 'Who the hell are *you*?' *That's* when I found out about my old man, and why he goes away, and *where* he goes too, 'cause she put her hand over the phone, you know, thinking I couldn't hear but I heard everything. She goes, 'Hey, Harrington, put your pecker in your pants one minute. There's a kid on the phone says he's your son.' Then I heard him say, 'How the hell he find me here for Chrissakes? Tell him I'm not here.' She must have shaked her head 'cause he went, 'Do like I say. Just tell him I'm not here. Tell him you never heard of me.' So she gets back on the phone and does like he says. 'He never heard of anyone named Harrington, this guy here. You got the wrong number. I thought you asked for somebody else.' So I don't say nothing. Like, I was so surprised I didn't know what the hell to tell her when she said that. All this time the nose is looking at me, like he's thinking, 'What the hell is going on over there? Who the hell you talking to anyway?' So finally I tell her, and I'm starting to cry now, man. I could feel myself crying all over the goddam phone, 'Tell my father I never want to see him again. Tell him he's chicken shit.' The cop thought I was kidding. He thought I was stalling for time, and the woman hung up in my face. Bam! Like that.

"But this cop with the nose, he was all right. He made me talk to him about my father. At first I didn't want to, but then I thought, why not, I ain't got anybody else here. I was sort of interested to know what I *would* say. What I said was that I was ashamed of him and he was ashamed of himself too 'cause he didn't have a job and he didn't have anyplace to go where people respected him, which I suppose was a lot like me too. He couldn't look at my mother so he found this other woman, Elaine knows her name. I knew it but I always want to forget it. He couldn't be a man with any of us. Like, he couldn't be a husband 'cause he didn't have any respect from my mother, 'cause she only respects men with lots of money. She's told me that herself. She said all the time I was growing up, 'I'll love you. I'll always love you. I'll always do that 'cause you're my own blood. But just 'cause I'm your mother don't mean I have to respect you. You got to earn that.' So when I'd ask her what do I have to do before I earn it—not that I could care one way or the other whether my old lady respected me because I don't think she's done so much in her life that I'd respect *her* for—she'd say, 'I'll probably never respect you. You ain't going to end up too much better than your father, and there isn't a soul anywhere who's going to respect *him*.'

"You see how this not working hit all of us. He didn't like himself 'cause he couldn't be a man with her. She told him after he'd been in and out of about, Jesus, seemed like a million jobs, until he got a steady job she wouldn't sleep in the same room with him. So he told her that wasn't fair. So she goes, 'You don't think it's fair? What about the rest of us with nothing to eat and no money for clothes and living in this lousy stinking place. Kids are always screaming for something *I* can't give them because *you* ain't got any job.' We heard 'em fighting all the time, but a lot of it was a lie because we never asked for nothing when he wasn't working. We knew what was going on. Even my little sister, every time she'd open up her mouth to ask for something, one of us would smack her or drag her out of the room. My parents saw what we were doing. We were only doing it to protect *them*, but my mother lied. She told him we were always asking for things.

"So there was my old man with no job and no wife. I guess he didn't have the courage to talk about his problems to the rest of us, which I don't blame him for, 'cause if I were in his shoes I wouldn't go blabbing off to my kids about what a failure I am. I mean, it'd be hard enough just looking in the mirror every day and seeing myself. That's the thing, I'm like that too. When I'm in trouble, or think I am, I start running away. Either I really do run away or my mind's working like I was running away. So my father finds this chick who likes him even though he's old and don't have a job. Maybe he never even told her he was married or did have a job or didn't have a job. I wouldn't blame him for nothing he did after the way my mother treated him. If you ask me, she should have stood by him, done everything he told her to do. She said she wanted to be with people she could respect, which is rich men. That's what she meant. She wanted a rich guy, which is a laugh. There ain't no trick to having respect for a guy with lots of bread. What the hell's so tricky about that? 'Course you like a guy who gives you everything you want. I would too. You know what I told her? I said she'd respect a rich guy but she wouldn't love him 'cause she'd be too busy taking things he gave her to love him. She'd say she loved him, but she wouldn't. If she had any guts she would have said to my father, 'Don't go running around when you don't have a job. Stay here, we'll take care of things. We'll think of something.' But no, she had to say, 'You got no job, then you ain't going to have no wife.' So how can I hate the guy when I'm feeling sorry for him half the time and wondering whether he's alive or dead the rest of the time. I told him to go to hell that time on the phone when I found him in bed with that woman, and I don't even know if I hated him then. The worst he is a creep, and nobody really hates a creep. They're just small little guys, little ants. Most of the time you're stepping on 'em, killing 'em, and you don't even know they're there.''

Eddie Harrington was detained in the precinct station eight and a half hours at the time of his first arrest. In the end, there was no formal investigation or charge, merely a severe warning that if there were a next time, the police would, as they said, come down hard on him, even though he was only fourteen years old. If the police had learned anything from the little bit of conversation with him, it was that he was an intelligent boy who knew the law and the penalties for breaking it. They had learned too that Eddie possessed an exceptional understanding of his parents' condition. They told him that this understanding should help him to be more compassionate with his parents, not cause them hardship by getting himself in trouble. It was a typical speech, Eddie reported, the sort of "Cop Sermon" every boy in the neighborhood had heard at one time or another. Yet in this case, there was something slightly out of the ordinary. On his way out of the precinct station that evening, as he waited for a policeman to drive him home, Eddie Harrington overheard a policeman say:

"That Harrington kid? You talk to him? Kid's sharp as a buck. Smartest kid Davies ever brought in here. But sick in the mind. I'll predict right now that boy will be in here one day with a murder charge wrapped around his neck. You hear him in there?"

Eddie claims he smiled when he heard this report on himself, but it terrified him too because he had been thinking a great deal of killing someone. There was no one in particular he wished to kill; it was only an urge that never subsided. Almost every day he would fantasize murder. He might be sitting on the trolley car coming home from school and he would see an elderly gentleman sitting across from him looking old, tired, depressed. He would imagine what the man's life was like and try to put himself in the man's body so that he could feel the heaviness and sadness he observed. At first he would feel sorry for the man and wish that he could help him, if indeed the man needed help. Then he would imagine having a conversation with the man, and a whole scene would unfold.

They would be traveling somewhere on the trolley. It would be night and only a few people would be riding in the car. Eddie would strike up a conversation, letting the man see his good-natured side.

"What do you say, Dad, how's it going with you?"

"Not bad, Son," the man would answer, obviously eager to talk with Eddie.

"But you look so glum, so down in the mouth. What you need is a good, stiff drink, or a night with a broad. Which is it?"

"Nah, that's not it," the man would protest with a grin, looking a bit sheepish. "Can't get a job, that's all."

"Is *that* all it is?" Eddie would ask, letting the man hear his most casual manner. "Hell, we can always find you a job."

"There ain't no jobs, Son. I've tried. Been trying for years to get one. Shoveling shit off the dock even, if they offered it to me. Got children to feed and a wife that still can stomach the sight of me. Got to find something, or I don't know what."

"Or what, Dad?" Eddie would get serious at this point and lean across the aisle to listen more closely.

"Or else, I'm going to have to leave the world, I guess. Ain't going to live this way no more. Can't take it. Family can't take it. Times are tough and all that, but that don't help me none. What happens to the next guy ain't none of my affair. It's only what happens to *me* that matters. I get a job I'm happy, or, I can make it for a while. Wouldn't say I'm happy exactly. Without a job, though, hell, I'll cut out of here."

They were the words his own father had spoken to him.

In his fantasy, Eddie would look shocked. "You'd kill yourself just 'cause you couldn't find a job?"

By this point both Eddie and the man would be glancing down the length of the car making certain no one was listening to them.

"Kill myself tonight if I knew no job was coming. Ain't worth going on for. Not enough to be alive. They say, long as you got your health you got it all, that's a crock, young man, a crock in the alley! You can make it knowing you're dying of some disease if you got something to do with yourself. It ain't the thought of dying that kills you, it's the thought that there ain't no sane reason in the world to get out of bed in the morning if you ain't got no job and you ain't got a person in the world who could give a running shit for you because you ain't got one. I know. I've been there more than once, more than twice; fact is, all the time now."

"And you're ready to die? Like now? Tonight?" At this point in the fantasy Eddie Harrington always did the same thing. Upon expressing his incredulity at the man's eagerness to die, he would try to compute his father's age, but he never could reach a figure that satisfied him. No matter how he reasoned, he invariably ended up making his father too old. Then he would determine to ask his father the next time he spoke with him, but he never did. He thought about the question when speaking with his father, but he never dared ask him directly.

"Listen, old man," he would say as his fantasy resumed, "I'm going to do you a favor, a favor of a lifetime."

The man would respond with almost childlike curiosity. "What you got?" And he would lean forward awaiting Eddie's proposition, Eddie could actually see him becoming youthful, content. His face would be transformed and his posture would change.

"I'm going to take that death problem away from you."

Still the eagerness and anticipation would gleam on the elderly man's face. He would look up at Eddie, as if the boy were twice his height. "But how?"

Then, as his hands began to perspire, his breathing quickened, his nostrils widened, Eddie Harrington would imagine himself becoming crazed with a sadistic passion. He would see himself standing up in front of the elderly man and producing a large, link-steel chain. He would yell at the few passengers in the car to get off and they would run away whimpering and screaming, covering up their faces for fear that Eddie would remember them and come looking for them. Then Eddie would begin to destroy the man. Starting with the man's legs, he would beat him with the chain, being careful that it would not whip around and smash him at the same time. With all his might he would swing the chain at the man's chest and hear the ribs crack and the man cry out in pain. Then he would use every muscle in his body to sling the chain so that it would not only crash against the man's skull, but wrap around it several times, splitting open the cheeks and the bones around the eyes and ears. Blood would pour out onto the seats and the floor of the car. The man would be soaked in blood, his face splintered and contorted in the ugliest way. And Eddie Harrington's heart would beat faster and faster until he could practically feel the pressure of his blood rising to the point of exploding. He would imagine that he was laughing and crying, swearing, yelling and whispering all at once. He would feel gratified and fulfilled, guilty and ashamed. And always the man's broken body would fall over frontward, thumping upon the dirty rubber matted floor of the trolley car and landing against Eddie's own legs in a sickening hulk. Eddie would kick himself free and want to vomit or urinate on the man. He would say aloud:

"There you are, old man. Lucky you aren't my real father. Now you don't have nothing to be sad about no more. Now you don't have to get up every morning wondering, do I have a job today or don't I? Will my wife and kids like me because I do have a job or I don't have a job? Now I don't have to look nobody in the face again and let 'em see what sort of a bum I really am. Rich man or beggar, they'll never know when they find me crushed to death. If I died for natural causes everybody would say he just quit 'cause he couldn't get work, chicken-shit son of a bitch. He could have found something if he really hunted for it. He found a chick didn't he, and he wasn't that young, you know, and he didn't have no money. Didn't even have a job, so how could he have money? Nobody's going to say that, or, 'I feel so sorry for his wife and his kids, 'specially that little boy of his. Ain't got no husband or father, now only because the man was a failure and a quitter, just like his wife always said he was.' No sir, they're going to find your body, my friend, all mangled up, and nobody's going to want to know whether you were a success or a failure, a good man or a bad man. All they're going to do is vomit when they see the kind of shape you're in and feel sorry for you. Fact is, they'll feel so sorry for you, they won't even bother to find out who you were. They might never know you're as poor as you are. Hell, they might even take you as being one of those rich guys, shelling out money to everybody, that my mother says she has so much respect for. So long, old man."

Eddie Harrington did not stop at setting fires in the safe confines of children's sandboxes. He didn't even stop at setting fires in places where serious conflagrations might have resulted. Once he was so frightened by a fire he started in a school yard several miles from his house—he had made a special trip to get there—that he telephoned the fire department. When they arrived Eddie concocted a detailed description of two boys who started the fire. The police were impressed by his description and asked his name, address, and telephone number. He gave them a false name and address and the telephone number of the woman his father visited. He never found out whether the police called her, but it would have made little difference to anyone if they had. She would say she never heard of Eddie Harrington or Bill Trent, the name he had contrived. It always impressed him that on the spur of the moment, and not without pressure, he had invented such a reasonable sounding name as Bill Trent. I'm going to be one helluva criminal, he thought, riding the trolley home after the fire at the Halliday School had been extinguished. There was, however, a real William Trent, someone Eddie Harrington knew about.

Eddie Harrington, Senior's last so-called steady job had been with the Amos Coal Company. He had told his wife the job looked secure. Money was tight in the coal industry and there would be layoffs coming, but the senior Harrington was not especially worried since he was high in the seniority ladder of the men in his department.

There were eight of them, and he was second in line behind the foreman. The entire department would be closed before the company laid off Ed Harrington. Besides, he had been a well-liked employee. Even Frank Amano said that Ed Harrington deserved to stay with Amos more than any other man, and everybody knew that Frank Amano never complimented anyone, especially someone with whom he was competing for a job. They told a story about Frankie Amano losing his job in a car plant in Michigan. When the news came he made inquiries and learned the names of the men who would be retained. When he discovered that three men he worked with were scheduled to be kept on, he broke the arm of one of them, threatened to kill him if he ever told what happened, and arranged to get reinstated in the company as a substitute. The men who despised Frank Amano said he was so ruthless he'd kill his own children if it meant his getting a job. The men who were terrified of Frank Amano said people get ruthless when they're out of work. It meant a lot to Ed Harrington when Frank Amano told him that he personally would make certain that Amos Coal would close its doors for good before they fired him.

Young Eddie was with his father the day the two men talked. He remembered Frank Amano as a tall, dark man with pitch-black eyes and the hairiest arms he had ever seen. He was afraid that Mr. Amano wanted to fight his father and relieved when it turned out they were friends.

"You like that guy?" Eddie Harrington asked his son after Frank Amano had driven off in a brand new Chevrolet. "Huh? What'd you think of him?"

Little Eddie didn't know what to say. Secretly he admired the dark, hairy man, although he was also afraid of him. But he sensed his father's attitude and shrugged his shoulders. "I don't know what do *you* think?"

"I'll tell you exactly," Ed Harrington told his son. "I love Frank Amano for one reason: I always know where I am with him. That's a great thing to know with another guy, just exactly where you are with him. When he says he's pulling for me and that this company will shut down before lose my job, I know he knows the place is in real trouble and he'd do everything in his power to keep me out of any job in this city if it looks to him like I'm standing in his way."

"That's what I thought," little Eddie answered, hiding his confusion, but not his admiration for his father.

"No it ain't," his father said suddenly. "You were taken in by him the same way I was. You believed every word he said. But you'll see what happens when he talks to Trent. Bill Trent got to be foreman 'cause he'd do anything anybody tells him. He's as big a liar as Amano is, only he don't have none of Amano's guts. Bill Trent's a phony. He's worse than Frank Amano because everybody walks over him. Even a kid your size could scare the piss out of him."

This was the conversation young Eddie Harrington remembered when the police asked for his name. Bill Trent, he had answered, for an instant unable to place the name. Then it came back to him. The walk with his father, his misjudgment of Frank Amano, his father's bitterness toward Bill Trent, and of course the end of the story, which was Bill Trent firing his father for reasons that were never explained. And then there was his father's parting lunch with Frank Amano and Bill Trent, and the two of them expressing their unhappiness and surprise, and promising to help Ed Harrington find another job.

Eddie Harrington remembers his father coming home that afternoon after the lunch and telling his mother how he was going into their savings to buy a gun. "What the hell do I have to lose any more?" his son heard him bellowing. "Might as well get a little bit of goddam satisfaction out of my life. Ain't had a fuckin' shred of it in forty years. I'd only be doing everybody coming up behind me a favor if I got rid of that son of a bitch Amano. Trent will choke in his own shit. Is anybody home?"

"Eddie," his mother had answered sharply.

The answer did not stop Ed Harrington. He went on railing against the men who had betrayed him.

"Miserable bastards," he had screamed. "You work your goddam ass off for years, for *years* goddamit, and what the hell does it bring you. They screw you behind your back, in front of your eyes. What the hell they give a goddam about? They care if you work? Dog eat dog out there? My ass. It's man eat man and those bastards always win. They'll win when I'm dead and buried too. They got two kinds of people in this world. They got suckers like me and they got the people who suck. Amano, Trent, all those bastards, they suck. They find people like me and they high-mouth us, every one of us. 'Oh, you'll get the job, Harrington. You'll be the first to stay, last to leave. You been here the longest, we'll give 'em all kinds of shit if they mess with you, Harrington, you little Irish asshole. We're rooting for you, Harrington. Standing up there next to you, behind you, in front of you, anywhere you want us to be 'cause you're our guy,

Harrington. You aren't alone in the world, Harrington. You got a family to feed. Nice wife, nice daughters, good-looking son. You got it made, Eddie baby, ain't no one going to touch you without coming through us first!'

"Miserable cock suckers. Chrissakes, that son of a bitch Amano was bullshitting me right in front of my kid. Right the fuck in front of my goddam *kid*. I asked him, two weeks ago, less than that, I asked him, 'Eddie, what'd you think of Frank Amano? What do you think of the man?' And the kid's taken in. He's ready to tell me he thinks Amano is God's fucking gift to the goddam human race. Frank Amano, baby, I know your kind. I can smell you out ten blocks away, half a fuckin' country away. You're in Detroit and you hear something's happening in Pittsburgh, you go, man. You eat people and you spit 'em out to take care of yourself. You want to know about Frank Amano and Bill Trent, who by the way is the biggest bullshitter 'cause his name is Grady, or O'Grady, and he's afraid some folks will steal his little goddam job from him if they find out he's a mick? So he passes. One day he's a little Irish Catholic, then you see him two days later and maybe he's a Presby or a Methodist, or whatever the hell he needs. Christ, he'd pass as a goddam Jew or nigger in blackface if he could save his job or take someone else's from him.

"You want to tell me times are tight, okay, times are tight. They've never been this bad. It's hitting everybody. Okay, so I'm just part of the great old American system. Okay, so now I know, so what the hell good's it going to do me? I got kids I got to feed. And what the hell is anybody, my family, anybody supposed to think when all they hear about is me losing my fucking job all the time? What the hell you supposed to say to them? 'Hey, Daddy, how come you ain't working and Frank Amano and Bill Trent are? Huh? How come that is? We see their kids, we play with 'em all the time. How come you're always home and their fathers are always working?' What do I say? They got someone going to give me a little advice about all that? Sure, they got things to tell you to say. You just say, 'Well, Son, I'll tell you what the story is. Come sit here on Daddy's lap and he'll tell you the facts of life. You see, Son, guys like Frank Amano and Bill Trent can be explained real simple. Say there was one job in the world left for a man to do and two people who might take the job. They're one of the guys, see, and the guy competing for the job is their own son. Now mind you, their son is just a newborn baby still in the hospital, two days old. They still got him there in one of those cribs 'til he's old enough to get out of the hospital. Just like they had you in when you were born. Frank Amano and Bill Trent would go into that nursery in that hospital, and thinking their boss just might go crazy and give the one job in the world to this little two-day-old kid lying there in his own piss and shit, they go in there and squeeze the little kid to death so they can make sure they got the job. Then they go right out, have a drink, and bring their goddam wife a bunch of flowers and a big card that says, 'Jesus Christ, Hon, you know how bad I feel. I wanted that little fellow in there just as bad as you did. I can't imagine what kind of animal could have done that to him.' "

Eddie Harrington, who had been curled up on his bed, the heels of his hands pressed against his ears in a futile effort to keep from listening, heard his mother cry out to his father:

"Jesus Christ, Ed, you're mad. You're really sick. They've made you sick, or the job thing has, or something has, and I don't give a damn what it is. But you are *sick*. And I forbid you to be near the kids when you're like this. You better get out of here. Jesus, you're mad. Killing a two-day-old baby. What the hell are you talking about? There's two kinds of people in the world all right, sick ones and healthy ones, and brother, I don't know much, but you sure as hell aren't one of the healthy ones. You're out of your mind. Killing babies? What the hell's with you? Get out. Get out!"

Young Eddie heard a chair fall over and a noise that sounded like someone being hit with a cushion. He was too terrified to open the door and see what his parents were doing, much less let himself imagine what they looked like in their fury. Suddenly, the door to his room flew open and his father was standing there. Ed Harrington looked surprised to find his son huddled on the bed, but not embarrassed.

"You hear?" he asked in a calm voice.

His son merely nodded.

"Good. Might be the best education about life you'll ever get. You hear the part about choking little babies?"

Eddie Harrington could not move. He could neither nod nor speak. His mouth was dry and the palms of his hands were covered with perspiration.

"You heard," his father said. "I'll tell you something else just to make certain you got it in your head for good." All the while he held the doorknob in one hand and the door frame in the other, his large fingers gripping tightly to the wood until the tips of his fingernails showed white crescents. "There's only one thing in life that matters, and that's working, working steady at whatever the hell you do. It ain't important whether you choose it or find it or stumble on it. All I know is you got to work, regular. Every day. Monday, Tuesday, Wednesday, Thursday, Friday. Saturday and Sunday too if you need the money. But you shouldn't have to if you put in an honest forty hours. And you fight for every job and fight to keep it as if they were trying to take away your two arms. You get it? Your two arms. Don't believe nobody. Listen to nobody. The only thing that talks is the job. When you got it you got everything. When you lose it, or when those bastards out there take it away from you, you got nothing. They can throw every word in the goddam dictionary at you and you still don't have nothing. You got that?"

Still his son did not move.

"Get a job, then get yourself a gun. A big one. Keep it with you loaded so the first guy that starts messing with you gets it right between the old eyes. Let 'em take your wife, your home, your car, anything they like, but die before they take your job away. 'Cause you're going to be like me, 'cause you're my blood.

And you're going to die the same way I do. With a job you got life; without it, you're long since dead. You get what I'm saying?''

Eddie nodded.

''I'll be back. Look after your mother.'' Ed Harrington, Senior, closed the door. His son heard the door to the outside open and close and his father slowly descending the concrete steps.

Ed Harrington's speech to his son had been perfectly direct, and delivered with calmness and strength. He knew exactly what he had wanted to say, almost as if he had been waiting for just that moment to say it. Yet, it was almost impossible to believe that he could have been as calm and straightforward when, throughout the talk, such heavy tears had flowed from his eyes. He must have known he was crying, but he didn't let that stop him. Perhaps this was because his son too had been crying, and there was no use for either man to speak about it.

At fifteen, not long after his birthday, Eddie Harrington was arrested by the police for stealing money from a grocery store. When taken to the police station he was also charged with setting fires on six different occasions. One of the fires he allegedly set had destroyed an old wooden building near the railroad tracks that had long been condemned and therefore vacated. As it happened, a little boy was playing in the building and perished in the fire. This meant that Eddie was also charged with involuntary manslaughter. He stayed in jail thirteen months awaiting trial. When at last his case was taken to court, the judge ruled that there was insufficient evidence to prove his role in the setting of four fires, but ample evidence to find him guilty of arson in the other two, as well as the robbery. He was sentenced to prison for a term to run no less than one year, no more than three years.

At the sentencing, the judge apologized to Eddie Harrington and his mother for the way the boy had been detained. Mrs. Harrington nodded as though accepting the judge's words. Eddie merely stood still, looking tough but beaten. When the judge asked Eddie whether his father was in the courtroom, Eddie answered quietly, ''No.'' When the judge then asked, ''Is your father alive?'' the boy thought for a conspicuously long time. His mother too remained silent. Finally he looked down and mumbled, ''I don't know. If he is, he wouldn't be here. He'd be out someplace looking for a job!''

__5__

A Young Man's Love

The high school ceremony in June was pleasant enough. There was singing, speeches, a valedictorian address by a young woman named Darcy McCullough, and a dance. The parents of the students exchanged congratulations and expressed hopes for the children they had known for so many years. Their own parents attended even though they were unhappy that their children would not be attending college. A young man and a young woman, graduates from a Denver suburban high school, had decided that what they wanted, for this moment in their lives, was to travel across the country and be together. They would be leaving in one month.

It was a fine plan, they were told by their friends on the night of graduation. The parents of these friends nodded agreement, but the young man and young woman could see that only a few people genuinely affirmed their trip, much less endorsed their ideals. Behind their backs they felt the others ridiculing them, laughing at their inevitable misadventures, and perhaps, too, begrudging them their freedom, if it could be called that. What a waste of an education, they imagined others saying. And what a sad evening this must be for their parents. All that investment in school, and leading to what? A trip across the country? Wouldn't a summer of travel be enough? How much are people meant to stand?

To anyone at the party who dared to ask them, the young couple spoke of their trip with modesty. They pressed their hands together and whispered messages and nonsense words that meant love and isolation from the others. They watched their parents trying to enjoy themselves and imagined they saw wrinkles of worry on their parents' faces. They saw disappointment, even in the looks of their younger sister and brother, both of whom wanted them to attend college, although they would never admit it. The young man and young woman had taken weekend trips into the mountains, backpacking into forest spaces. They loved these days together with the land. If their love was truly strong, they said again and again, then nothing could be more important than living together. And so they planned to travel with each other, and, as they said, with their country. Those of us from the mountains, the young woman always said, must see the oceans and know the people of the oceans.

Even in their isolation, the couple was pleased that so many classmates would come to them, extending good wishes and asking that they send them postcards from famous cities. Many of their friends disapproved of their trip; they already assumed the attitudes of their parents and teachers. Their hypocrisy, the young man often said, was one of the reasons for taking this journey.

It's a lie, he thought, watching the dancers, his parents, and his younger sister. Everybody preached honesty and fairness, but honesty and fairness were not among their values when they made important decisions. All of them cheated in one way or another. They hurt people. So did my parents.

The young man observed his father speaking to the teacher. His father appeared interested, amused. Such false charm, the young man thought bitterly. I hate him for being there, and for being my father. There isn't a father in this room that matters to any children. Girls love their fathers because they don't have to live with them. It's easy for a father to love his daughter because he'll never let her work with him. But fathers destroy their sons. They're scared that their sons will be better than they are and nowhere as good as they are at the same time. This is no rebellion, my trip with her. I haven't enough interest in him to get my energy up to plan a rebellion, the sort of rebellion he ought to feel.

There was always a sense of distance, of coldness with his father. He always thought that if there ever was a time when his father was asked to save him from a dangerous situation, his father might very well let him die. "Men are meant to be independent and self-sufficient," he would imagine his father saying. Or perhaps he would say, "Just put yourself in my shoes, son, and tell me honestly you wouldn't act the same way I did." His father might rescue him, but even the most dramatic life-saving experience would not lessen the distance between them. And as if this feeling were not saddening enough, the young man wondered whether he, having somehow inherited his father's qualities, didn't feel the same way toward·people he claimed to love.

The night before his graduation, the young man dreamed that he and some friends are travelling somewhere near the North Pole. It is freezing cold, even during the day when the sun shines. They walk across hilly land covered with snow. The wind covers over their footprints with snow. For warmth, they lie naked, wrapped together in their clothes, but the young man feels pain. He knows he will die in the snow and never be found and the young woman will survive. Despite the freezing cold, he moves his toes. He discovers that he is wearing his father's army boots. Then he cries.

The huge gymnasium was decorated with flowers and streamers of gold and blue, the school's colors. The rows of benches that normally stood on one side of the room had been dismantled and stacked in one corner. In the dim lighting they looked a bit like a small city, low buildings huddled together.

The young man imagined a time when he was six. He is with his father sitting at the dining room table after Sunday morning breakfast. Sections of the newspaper are scattered about on the floor. He and his father have made room for themselves to work at one end of the table. They are building a model of an animal. It is a deer or a horse, he cannot remember exactly. He remembers feeling his father's hand touch his own. The touch makes him feel excited. Then he and his father are gluing pieces of the animal together. When they come to the pelvis he watches his father apply the glue. He notices a hole where the animal's genitals should be. His father grins, studying the directions and hunting in the box for pieces that might have been mislaid. "I guess that's the way they want this animal to go into the world," his father says. The young man keeps his face expressionless, letting his father believe he has not understood the remark, but he feels embarrassed.

Thoughts of his parents had been on his mind ever since Thanksgiving when he telephoned them. He missed not being home. At first his parents had sounded lonely for him. It was as though they were forgetting the other children and thinking only of him. He refused to admit to himself that he liked their special attention. His father had missed him. The very trip his father had so opposed and which had made him ashamed at the graduation ceremony was causing his father to miss him.

The young man poured paint from one can into another and began painting the door on the last cottage. He stepped back to inspect the long line of doors.

My father will die someday, he thought, and there I'll be, never having told him a thing. But he's to blame. Everyone who knows the family knows that. The man doesn't have a friend in the world. The guy that parks his car is probably his closest friend, and my parents would never invite that guy to dinner. He's pathetic, my old man. The relationship is pathetic. He can't be anything but cold, and I've run away. That's all it is. Every kid wants to know whether he's adopted and every kid wants to run away.

The young man was overcome with a desire to return home. He wished to be with his parents, warmed by them, wanted by them. He wished that he could be in the midst of a family scene in which people openly loved and gave to one another, and no one felt ashamed by what they were saying. It could be a Christmas scene, with food and presents; his returning, his very being in his parents' house would be his present. He could surprise them, for there were still five days in which to reach Denver. He could act casually when he arrived, as though he could take or leave the whole business. Let them make the efforts, let them explode with feelings in which he might revel, let them forgive him.

He wished also that his parents would honor his trip, even reward it.

Perhaps if they did he might end it and content himself with his almost six months on the road. After all, he had had a significant experience, what more was left to be discovered. He wished that his parents would see him as the favorite child, and not merely because he was returning. At least let him be his father's chosen son, the one with whom he shared the most, the one whose life most clearly gratified his father's secret desires.

What was clear to the young man was how he wanted his father to respond to him as a mother normally responds to a child. He wanted sentimentality and open affection—a display of precious moments, like jewelry, to sanctify their involvement. In wishing for his father to behave in a certain manner, he found himself dreaming of becoming his father and thereby making it possible for his mother to be treated with the tenderness and strength that his father had never shown her.

The young man imagines himself returning home. There is snow on the ground; it is Christmas. He rings the front door bell, although he knows where his parents hide an extra key.

His hair and coat are covered with snow and he carries presents, each of them beautifully wrapped. His parents answer the door. They are shocked to see him. His mother takes the presents and embraces him. His father begins to shake his hand, then, feeling foolish and uncomfortable, hugs him. It is a wonderful family reunion. The house is freshly cleaned and the smell of the Christmas tree fills every room. His mother has been baking little chocolate cakes and vanilla cookies with coconut frosting on them. Freshly candied orange peels have been placed in a large bowl which drips with sugar. His parents offer him something to eat, but he refuses.

"When did you get in?" they ask.

"Oh," he answers casually, "I've been in town for several days."

"But you didn't call," his mother says.

The young man's father presses his wife's arm, a silent warning not to make their son explain. The young man smiles and admits he was joking. "Just got in," he announces. "This minute. You think I'd be in this part of the country and not come and see you first thing?"

His parents are relieved. They look at him lovingly and insist that he try the Christmas sweets. He resists at first, but then takes a handful of orange peels and cookies, which are still warm. His younger sister follows him everywhere, looking at him admiringly. His older brother is in the house but does not come to meet him.

Soon the family is sitting in front of the fireplace. The young man has chosen the chair his father always sits in, leaving his father to sit on the arm of the couch. His father, radiant with happiness, begs the young man to recount every detail of the trip.

"I hate like hell to admit it," his father says, "but all my life I wanted to take a trip like you did. What a trip it must have been. Ten years since we've seen you. Not a card or a letter in all that time, not even a telephone call. Yet I knew you were well. A father knows. They always say a mother knows instinctively when something is wrong with her children, even when they're miles away. Well, I don't know much about instincts and mothers, but I knew you were fine. I don't have those kinds of feelings about your sister and brother. Don't know why I don't but I don't. But I have them about you. And if I didn't before you left, I surely have them now. I want you to know, son, and I promise you this is the last time I'll mention it, I thought about you every hour you were gone. Morning, noon, and night.''

"Don't you think you're laying it on a bit heavily?'' his mother asks.

"I'm sure I am,'' his father says. "But this is my son, my favorite child. If I don't tell *him* these private thoughts, who in the name of God do I tell?''

The young man, like his mother, is put off by his father's sentimentality, but hopes nonetheless that his father will continue. He sits on his father's favorite armchair nibbling at cookies and admiring the presents everyone has received. His parents, while not knowing he would return home after ten years, have bought Christmas presents for him. Among them is a set of history books with glorious pictures of the midwest and east coast. There is also a new pair of hiking boots and a handsome green wool sweater. It fits him perfectly.

"You know,'' his father says softly, "ever since you went away, I put a picture of you in a locket and have worn it around my neck.'' His father unbuttons his collar and reaches down under his shirt to pull out the locket. No one in the family has known of the locket. His father puts his fingernail in the crack of the locket and opens it, revealing a handsome picture of the young man. Opposite the picture is a tiny frame for another picture. The frame has been left empty. "I suppose I could have put anybody's picture there,'' his father explains, "but truthfully, there was no one I could think of who merited a place beside my son. Not even my own parents. How do you like that?'' he laughs, reaching out to squeeze the young man's hand.

"Really,'' his mother says as if scolding her husband and her son. "This is going on too long if you ask me.''

"We'll talk privately when no one is around,'' his father promises. "Problem with this family is that no one lets anybody love anybody freely, man to man even, like families are supposed to.''

"That's why I took this trip,'' the young man says.

"I know it. Don't think in all those months when I was just too damned proud to give you my approval for it, that I didn't know what you had up your sleeve. I knew why you had to do it. I knew you planned that trip the minute you planned it. Did you know that?''

"That's awfully good, Pop.''

"Well, I don't know about it being awfully good, but I knew it. Fathers know. Some things boys do that men just understand.''

The young man is pleased to see how much his father has changed and how willing he himself is to share things with his father. The trip has brought out the youth in his father, a quality he has never before seen. For the first time he feels close to both his parents, but there is a special attachment to his father.

The young man painted carefully around the hinges and knob of the last cottage door. If no more snow fell, his next job would be painting the window frames on the cottages. He dreaded this task, for it required him to work slowly with a small brush around the casings and along the diagonal splines.

The scene of his home and Christmas returned. His father still sits on the couch, leaning toward him as if reminding him that the two of them share an important secret.

"Say," his father says, "here we are pushing you to talk about your trip and we haven't even asked you once about that young woman you were traveling with. It's been so long since you started that trip, I can barely recall her face. I remember her being a nice young lady, perfect partner for you on the venture." His father winks at him, "How'd she make out? Was she able to keep up with you? I know I couldn't keep up with you even when I wasn't as old as I am now." He smiles kindly.

"You aren't ill, are you, Dad?" the young man asks. His manner shows concern.

"I'm not all that well, son."

"Have you seen a doctor?"

"Of course."

"What's the doctor say?"

"I don't think this is the best time for this discussion," the young man's mother intervenes. "Why don't you two save that for later. Tell us about the young woman."

The young man looks at his father who nods, as if to say, you and I can talk later.

"Well," the young man begins, "the young woman is not too good, I'm sorry to report. She kept up, no problems there. Fact is, she led me a merry chase more than I led her. Strong woman, you know."

"Got to do that," his father agrees.

"So I give up trying to find out, although inside I'm angry. It's killing me that I can't know, but I keep it inside. It's like, when you have that anger and uncertainty living inside it will kill you."

"It's what's killing me," his father whispers.

"What do you mean, Dad?" the young man asks with fright.

"Later. There will be time later."

"You mean about your illness?"

"Your father is dying from anger and uncertainty that he has carried inside him all his life," the young man's mother announces flatly, "but he'll tell you himself."

There was a time once, he remembered, when his family had a snowball fight in the street in front of their house. The city had been hit by a tremendous snowfall during the night, and the following morning his father had challenged the children to a snowball fight. The young man could not recall a time when the family had seemed as happy. He remembered the children shrieking with delight as they ran around the house, which in his memory seemed so large, hunting for gloves, snow boots, and scarves. They played in the middle of the street, for the snow had made the roads impassable. Schools had been closed and everyone in the world, it seemed, was outside walking about or having snowball fights.

The young man remembered his father throwing snowballs at the children. His father had seemed very strong, but he threw the snowballs gently to make certain no one would be hurt. Once the young man hit his brother in the forehead with a snowball. Steaming mad, his brother had run after him, pushing his face in the snow. His father intervened protecting the young man and admonishing his older brother to be a good sport and to remember that he was older and bigger. His brother said his father was unfair. His father said fairness is in the eyes of the judge.

Moments later, his father walked beneath a tall spruce tree in the neighbor's yard only to have a flurry of snow fall on his head. Everyone laughed, especially the young man's mother, but the young man felt sad and embarrassed for his father.

The young man remembered nothing of the surgery. He barely remembered the two men lifting him into the rear of the ambulance and the sound of the siren. He had no memory of entering the hospital or being wheeled into the operating room. Appendicitis and peritonitis had doubled him up with pain. Some people had administered to him all the pain killing pills they could find but nothing had helped, except the hours of fitful sleep which alternated with protracted periods of semi-consciousness and crying. At last someone ran to the police station. An ambulance hurtled him through the strange city in its blackest hours. He was operated on at four o'clock in the morning, the surgery being performed without complications.

When he awoke from the anesthetic, he found himself in a small room almost completely empty of everything except a row of beds, none of them with matresses on them. The only other objects in the room were three tall gas tanks, painted red, blue, and black. They stood near his bed like a trio of surrealistic clowns but they made him think he had been shoved into the hull of a ship. On the glass door he saw the words Recovery Room. After six hours he was wheeled on a cart to a ward which he shared with four other men, one of them a young man who had been stabbed in the lung during a fight. Lenny Pangione could not have been more than sixteen years old, and his long flat curvy nose looked as though it had been broken at least once every year of his life. His skin was dotted with pimples and his hair seemed excessively greasy. He combed it incessantly although clearly the effort of raising his arms above his shoulders caused him pain. The best thing about Lenny Pangione was that he acted as if nothing in the world could ever bother him. "A stab in the lung, a stab in the heart," he would say, "big deal. So what. Long as I got my teeth." Then he would grin and show his most prized features, his absolutely perfect teeth. And he had never once, so he claimed, visited a dentist.

After a week in the hospital, the young man was visited by his friend, Joan. She had been the one who ran to the police station. She wanted to know if he had spoken with his parents.

"They would only worry," he said. The young man thanked her and asked her about his friends at the house. Everyone was fine, she said, although no one had seen his young woman for several days.

"I thought she would have visited you by now."

"She did," the young man lied.

"You need anything?" Joan asked with her usual kindness.

"Nothing at all."

"No pain?"

"No pain."

"Have a Happy New Year then," she said before leaving. "A good life too."

"You moving?" he asked.

"To California."

"Take me with you."

"You have a woman." She waved good-bye.

When Joan left the room the young man wept. He turned in his bed so that Lenny and the other men could not see his face. He longed to call his parents and have them come for him. The telephone was on a table no more than two feet from his hand but he could not allow himself to reach for it. He sought to comfort himself by imagining the call to his parents he would not make.

"Hello, Dad?"

"Yes."

"It's me."

"Son, where are you?"

"That's a little hard to say."

"What do you mean? Are you all right?"

"Fine, no trouble."

"You're lying, son."

"Why do you say that?"

"I sense you're ill. I'm coming to see you."

"I'm fine, Dad. Never been better."

"You in a hospital, son?"

"Hospital? What makes you think I'd be in a hospital?"

"I just know. Call it men's intuition. Call it mysticism."

"Mysticism? Bunk."

"Call it bunk. Where are you, son? In the midwest someplace?"

"What makes you say that?"

"It's the New Year. I figured you for Chicago about this time. Why didn't you write?"

"I started to, Dad, but . . ."

"I understand, son. No matter. Where are you, Chicago? Hammond? Whiting? I'll bet it's Gary. Is it Gary?"

"Just what makes you say Gary?"

"I feel it in my bones. You're sick in a hospital in Gary, Indiana, right?"

"Sick? Hospital? Gary, Indiana? No one's ever sick in a hospital in Gary, Indiana, Dad."

"Then you're the first one, son. I'll be there in two hours. I'll be on the next plane to Chicago unless I can charter a plane direct to Gary."

"Charter a plane? Dad, you're crazy. Where are you flying to? I'm fine."

"What was it, son? Appendix? Ruptured appendix? Something like that?"

"A ruptured *what*?"

"You find yourself urinating blood, son?"

"Urinating blood? What are you talking about? I told you I'm perfectly . . ."

"I think there's a direct flight to Gary. I'll be on it. You want me to bring something for you?"

"Dad, you're losing your mind, I'm fine. Nothing's wrong. Honest."

"I'll bring your blue bathrobe. Just what you need for walking around the hospital."

"I'm not in a hospital."

"Do you have a good doctor, son? First class guy?"

"What do you mean, doctor?"

"What about your room? Private? Ward? What have you got there?"

"I'm not in a hospital room. I'm as healthy as I've ever . . ."

"They don't have you convalescing in the hall or in some nurses station, for God's sake, do they?"

"Nurses station? Dad, you're running away with yourself."

"It's a ward, huh? What have they got three, four other guys in there with you?"

"Other guys in *where* with me, Dad?"

"You know something, son, getting information out of you is like yanking a tooth out of a hippo. You've always been that way. All right, let's see. Ruptured appendix, blood in the urine, abdominal pains precede the operation by a week or two, maybe more, a ward room in a Gary Indiana hospital. I've got your blue bathrobe, maybe I'll bring some slippers, too, there's always a draft on those floors. Some good books. I can buy something at the airport. You still love science fiction, son?"

"Sure, but I don't have time to read. I'm well."

"Science fiction it is then. Direct flight to Gary. Any trouble getting a cab out there?"

"Where are you going in a cab? Dad, what's come over you?"

"You know something, son, I'd rather ask questions of the Internal Revenue Service or the CIA. At least I'd get 'no comment' or *something* from *them*. You're lucky I love you as much as I do or I'd never have figured this stuff out. You there, son?"

"Sure."

"So quiet, I didn't know if you hung up on me."

"I'd never do that, Dad."

"Good boy. What's your hospital room number?"

"809."

"809 it is. See you within two hours. Hang on, son, you'll make it."

"I'm making it, Dad. I'm making it."

"Just be brave, boy."

"What's with your voice, Dad? There's something wrong with the connection all of a sudden?"

"Nothing wrong with the connection. I'm crying. So long, son."

"Hey, Dad?"

"Yes."

"Could you hurry?"

6

A Painful Voyage

The story of Jack Adrian, a machinist with an automotive firm, a man who seemed to have more personalities than money, as his mother-in-law said over and over again, is not altogether unfamiliar to psychiatrists, psychologists, and social workers. The son of a carpenter's assistant who never seemed able to pull together enough money to buy a home, Jack Adrian, as they say, came up the hard way. He lived through difficult times, fell in and out of friendships, usually because people were unable to put up with his mercurial ways one day and his abject moodiness the next. "To know old Jack," his brother once told me, "is to know a half dozen guys, a hundred, for all I can count." The mood swings also never stood him in good stead at school. Teachers were either having to reprimand him for his verbal or physical outbreaks, or asking his parents about Jack's sudden quiet ways and shyness. The family was perplexed. What the boy made of his own moods is something nobody ever discerned. Either he was too angry to talk about it, or he withdrew into himself.

"The guy's nuts!" That's what they would say. The teachers, principals, friends, relatives, everybody. "Nuttier than a fruitcake." Here today, gone tomorrow, a natural for the loony bin. Perhaps he was a "natural" because of the daily scenes he encountered at home. His parents, apparently, were constantly fighting—at least they did when they weren't drinking. His brothers and sisters had not the slightest interest in caring for him, even though, as the youngest child, he was placed in their care a part of every day. Said simply, although one hesitates to reduce a man's problems to one single issue, Jack Adrian grew up believing not only that he was unlovable, but that his very being engendered distrust if not open hatred. It wasn't that people had given up on him, for that would be to suggest they once did believe in him. If the accounts of friends and relatives are correct, Jack Adrian just grew up yearning for love, but distrusting anyone who might have wanted to show him the slightest morsel of it.

The years between his sixteenth and twenty-first birthdays were shakey ones. He had quit school at fifteen. His father died when he was eighteen leaving his mother, physically weak and exhausted from years of heavy drinking, with debts she would never be able to pay. On the trip home from the funeral she harangued against her dead husband, blaming him for the world's evils and making certain that her son Jack knew that if he failed in business as miserably as his father, he had better not show his face in her house again. When he turned to his brothers riding with them in the car, their looks indicated they felt exactly as their mother did, even though neither of them were what anybody would call successful.

A long and complex story is shortened by noting that on his twenty-first birthday Jack Adrian took it upon himself to throw a party. He invited as many people as he believed could fit into his mother's apartment where he lived at the time. Most of the guests never showed up, but one who did, Sally Fuerst, more than made up for the absent ones. She was the first person to take a genuine interest in Jack Adrian; the first person, as it turned out, who showed him love, no matter what he gave her in return. It wasn't pity, she assured him repeatedly; it was merely old fashioned love. It took him a while to get adjusted to this sort of treatment, but gradually his personality seemed to change, and he was the first to attribute what he called "the cure" to Sally. They were twenty-four years old when they got married, and the fact that Jack's mother was too drunk and one of his brothers too busy to attend the wedding didn't seem to phase him. It was more important, he told his wife, that *her* parents come, which they did.

Sally Fuerst Adrian never conceived of the relationship with her husband in terms of psychological rehabilitation. She never used words like that, nor thought in those terms. She didn't fall madly in love with Jack at the birthday party. Her most powerful recollection of that evening was that he seemed sad. She never believed, moreover, that he was an angry or depressed man. Somewhere among all the changing personalities was a decent man, not to mention a man who had been hurt often in his life and never had felt the warmth of simple kindness. "Don't make anything dramatic out of it," she told me when I first heard about the Adrians' courtship. "I liked him at first. No, at first I was a little afraid of him. Then I liked him, then I couldn't tell, then I decided just because *he* was afraid to love me or anybody *I* didn't have to be afraid. It's not a plot for the movies. You don't really change people, at least I don't think so. You just bring out the good stuff in them and try to keep them from being so over-involved with their bad stuff, the stuff they like the least in themselves. And don't kid yourself, Jack did a lot for me too. I'm not his nurse!"

Now I jump ahead, way ahead in the story of Jack and Sally Adrian. I jump, in fact, over twenty years to the time when I met the family, knowing, of course, nothing of their personal histories. In retrospect, if I were to characterize those first few years of my friendship with the Adrians, I would say it was remarkable that their respective histories almost never cropped up in conversation. I knew that Jack's parents were dead, that he had little to do with his brothers and sisters, and that both the Adrians always had been closer to Sally's side of the family. I knew too that Jack reached a level of success that far exceded his parents' expectations. The home, the car, the two-week vacations were hardly a part of his own childhood. But of his mood swings—the battles with his parents, his father's pessimistic outlook of two decades earlier—I knew nothing. Neither of the Adrians seemed to be secretive people. They were loving with their four children, though uncompromising when it came to discipline. They tended to judge themselves, moreover, strictly in terms of how well their children were faring. What I could not quite piece together was their concern that one of their children might begin to show the dreaded mood shifts that had dominated Jack Adrian's early years.

While the Adrians never spoke to me of it, they clearly kept close watches on their children, fearing that Jack's mental "illness" might have been inherited by his children. Again, I could understand their concern, although no one who new the four Adrian children would have imagined they might be heading for psychological problems. They were lovely, talkative children with energy to spare. They adored the "right" foods, television shows, football and baseball teams, and rock songs. They fought with each other, and looked after one another, like all children. They didn't even seem to change that much when their father, wholly unexpectedly, grew increasingly depressed during his fifty-fifth year. Sally worried, but if the children were upset, they revealed it to no one, not that their parents asked them to verbalize their reactions. No one talked much about "it," even when Jack found himself making little or no progress in psychotherapy. Then a series of drugs was prescribed, some of which seemed to bring him back to an even keel. With the drugs, however, the children began to take increasingly more notice of their father. Part of their concern, naturally, were the side effects. First he was awake and alert. Then he would be quiet and lethargic for several days, to the point where he would stay in bed. Occasionally the children found him weeping.

To say the least, Jack Adrian's psychological state was not helping his position at the automotive firm. In the beginning, absences were overlooked, but being out of work for weeks at a time was not tolerated. The more his employers questioned his behavior the more angry and nervous he became. Eventually the Adrians decided not to answer their telephone during the daytime. Given Jack's condition, Sally grew conflicted around the issue of whether she should retain her own job as a secretary or stay home and nurse her husband, although she would never have used that term. She despaired seeing him unhappy and unconsolable, yet the family's financial problems would hardly be resolved with both of them sitting home. She made the obvious choice and continued to work. She also discussed the possibility of hospitalizing Jack, although he fought the idea tooth and nail. He'd get better, he kept saying. He had been in the depths before—not that he and Sally spoke much about connections between present problems and his early history.

Whatever their decisions, the Adrians appeared to be dealing with their problems as sensibly and, if you will, nobly as any one would dare expect. Privately, I took exception to one of their decisions: namely, their attempt to keep "the problem" from their children. Once again I was encountering what had now become a familiar family irony: the concealing of the unconcealable. How could people believe they could mask the mental illness of a father when the man was missing increasingly more days of work, staying in bed increasingly more hours a day, and showing himself to be increasingly more incapable of handling the normal responsibilities of everyday life? But of course this wasn't the predicament facing Mr. and Mrs. Adrian. Their problem was to keep neighbors, as well as Jack's *and* Sally's employers from hearing of Jack's illness. This meant stopping any leaks, which in turn meant keeping the truth, the *obvious,* from their children. This part of the story I understood only too well. Often it seems as though people's reactions to a mentally ill person is more severe than the patient's condition itself. Furthermore, the stigmatization of patients, as if they required further evidence of their lack of self worth, turns back upon them and probably perpetuates the illness. Could Jack Adrian's employment status be jeopardized if people learned of his condition? In Jack Adrian's world, the world of people who shared his fate, situations most definitely are damaged by mere gossip; so these people are not acting strictly in *paranoid* fashion—that overworked term—when they express a need to keep their problems inside the family, and away from their children.

As it happened, three of the Adrian children were adjusting fairly well to their father's troubles. They acted, in other words, as if simultaneously they knew and knew nothing of the matter. Thus, they were behaving exactly as their mother had instructed. It was a case of the Emperor's new clothes: if the parents said things were normal, then things were normal. But William Adrian, age fifteen, the third oldest, a boy who since early childhood had been called Chico, found himself unable to abide by the family's charade. He became, in a sense, the little boy who cries in "The Emperor's New Clothes," except that his proclamation was made in private, to me. Chico Adrian wouldn't buy the story. The earlier phrase about not swallowing the lie more accurately describes his feelings. After several months of watching his father sit in a chair for hours without uttering a sound and suddenly beginning to cry, Chico decided to stop eating. And it wasn't just liver, cottage cheese and jello that went off his list. The boy practically had to be forced to drink water. Occasionally when he consented to go with me on walks or car rides I got him to at least sip at a chocolate milkshake. I even worked out a foolish little game wherein the winner or loser had to munch pieces of a candy bar. "You're a fraud," he'd say. "All you're trying to do is get me to eat.'' ''I'm no fraud,'' I'd tell him. ''There's nothing mysterious about me at all. If I could I'd shove it down you. I can't stand to see you like this.''

If only to please me he would nibble at a sandwich or drink the milkshake. His older brother Ronald had a bit of luck with him as well, but his mother and two sisters had absolutely none. Not only did he refuse to take food from them, he complied with none of their demands. Still, given what the Adrians were going through, I felt that if only one child was visibly suffering, the family was coming out better than I imagined it would. Moreover, if we could keep Chico's problem under control, then surely everyone was ahead of the game.

Ahead of the game or not, the family went on this way for months. Sally Adrian was pleased that I spent time with Chico, but irritated by my desire to visit with Jack. In time she discouraged me from coming to the house, except to pick up Chico. Thus, I didn't know Jack Adrian had been admitted to a mental hospital until weeks after the decision had been made. I had a clue that something was worse than usual when I learned from Ronald that Chico had revealed a new symptom. This one consisted of him beating up on small children at school for no apparent reason. At first the teachers were surprised; aggression was not a quality Chico Adrian had ever demonstrated. But surprised or not, school officials could not condone it. The family was apprised of the situation and then warned that if the boy continued to act as he had, a suspension would ensue.

I learned all of this third hand; I learned of the actual suspension third hand as well. Chico told me nothing, until one afternoon when apparently he could hold his feelings no longer. As it turned out, he had heard the night before that his father would not be coming out of the hospital the following weekend as the children had been led to believe. Well, the words are not quite accurate. Chico had been told by his mother that his father would not be ''coming home from his long trip.'' There still had been no talk of hospitalization. Sally Adrian had not altered her original edict: mental illness and Jack's placement in a state hospital were not matters one discussed in front of the children. In response to his mother's edict, Chico had vowed he would never talk to her about his own suffering. In fact he vowed he would never speak to *anyone,* but the feelings burst through all the same:

''My mother's crazy. I believed her stuff about why you couldn't tell anybody. But she's treating us like babies. That's what she wants us to be, her babies, or a bunch of puppies. What's she so afraid of? *I'm* the one who should be afraid. I'm becoming a murderer almost. I hit a kid a couple of weeks ago. He didn't even do anything and I hit him. Hard too. You should have seen the way he looked at me. I could tell what he and his friends were thinking too. They were thinking: Adrian, you are weird, man. You must have pretty weird parents too if you come out weird like that. I don't know what to do. I don't know what to do.''

Chico Adrian's eyes were filling with tears which he fought back bravely. I had seen him sad before, but until this moment he had always been able to keep his eyes (deceptively) clear.

"She's got to face it, and *he's* got to face it. Everybody, you know, grows up wondering if they're, like, all right in their mind. You got to wonder about that. No one talks about it, but they'll make fun of it, so you know they're thinking about it. My father did, my mother did. My sisters wouldn't admit it but they do too. You gotta! You know how many days we had to tiptoe around the house pretending there was nothing wrong with him when you could *see* he was crazy. He wasn't my father, he was this crazy man, sitting in that chair staring at like nothing. He'd look at me and I'd think, he knows me, he doesn't know me. He knows me, he doesn't know me. You couldn't tell. I mean, I really couldn't tell if he even knew *he* was sitting there. And my mother, what does she say? 'Oh, Dad's a little under the weather,' or something unbelievable like that. Under the weather? I couldn't even have told you if the man could see or was he blind! That's when I decided I don't give a damn no more. I might just as well die. He doesn't know me, she's pretending like all he has is an upset stomach; maybe what he needs is a Dristan and he'll know his own son again. What kind of crazy shit is that? I'd go right up to him and say, 'Dad, you know me?' He didn't even move. Or he'd turn his head away like someone was shining a light in his eyes. And his eyes were dead. I can't explain it better. If he knew me it was only because I *pretended* he did. I was pretending my own father knew his son. I was afraid to ask him my name. I didn't even want to hear what he'd say."

"So, I decided I'm not going to live to have this hanging on my head. Someone in this house is crazy. It's him, her, or me, but one of us is way around the corner. I'm no doctor, so I don't understand what's happening. No one's ever sat down to explain it. I told my mother, 'Okay, look, since you don't want to tell me what's going on, let Tom Cottle tell me.' She got so mad you wouldn't even believe it. My father was sitting there. That was one of the nights when he'd, like, stare without blinking for a hundred hours. She told me, 'You are not now or *ever* to talk to Tom Cottle about this, your father, me, *anything*!' So why do I see him? I goes. She goes, he likes talking to you and buying you food, that's fine, but he doesn't have to know all our family's secrets. And she was really mad then. My father didn't even move. She was yelling and her face was turning red and he wasn't even moving. So I goes, he isn't supposed to hear no family secrets? Then all right, why doesn't someone tell *me* the family secrets. Is he going to die? That's what I wanted to know. I mean, no one ever told me nothing so I didn't know. He could have been dying. If anyone saw him like that they'd think he was dying. If you don't know, how you going to be able to tell?

"You should have seen her—yelling! I practically could see the smoke coming out of her head. 'Don't you dare say that. You father isn't dying. He's going to be absolutely fine.' 'When?' That's what I asked her. *When*? 'When he's ready.' I goes, 'Is that what the doctor said?' She goes 'What doctor?' 'Well, if you know so much you must have seen a doctor.' I scared her. I could see I did too, 'cause then I knew a little something. She doesn't want no doctor seeing my father. She wants to take care of him herself. When I asked her that question she got scared 'cause she thought maybe a doctor did come and see him once when she was at work which would have meant someone in the family told someone not in the family how my old man was sitting all day in his chair looking through people. Now why'd I go and call him my old man? I hate the word. He ain't that; he's my father.

"I used to kiss my father. Lots of boys don't but I did. He'd say, 'come kiss me goodnight,' something like that, and I would. I did it a little when he got sick. I call it sick no matter what she calls it or wants me to call it. I'd see him sitting all by himself, 'cause even if one of us was home we wouldn't talk to him 'cause she said there was nothing to be talked about—so, she wanted to pretend, we pretended. If your father wants to sit all day staring into space, you pretend *everybody's* father's sitting home all day staring into space. She said pretend but it was more like she really meant for us to ignore him. In the beginning I'd talk a little with him, and maybe when I'd go to bed I'd kiss him. Sometimes he'd move his head, like there was a bright light there or something. I don't know. But then I stopped. I'd think, 'One of us in this house is crazy. Either he's dead and I'm kissing a corpse, or something really strange is happening.'

"No one had to tell us something was wrong. We aren't children. And we aren't blind. I got to thinking that worse than he was was the way she was making us live with it; everybody was lying about it one way or another. I didn't want to eat. I figured out it wasn't really 'cause I wanted to starve myself to death. I just remembered my father telling us how his father would say, 'You don't deserve to eat if you haven't told the truth that day.' It was like even if you were the only person who knew you'd lied, you had to punish yourself. Maybe that's what I did. People like you making me eat only made it worse because it was like you were saying, 'You don't have to punish yourself,' which means you really aren't lying. But I was, and so was she. And if you want to know the truth, I thought *he* was the biggest liar of them all. Like, I'd see him sitting there, or lying down, and I'd think, he's putting us on; this is a fake. Something's *really* crazy; my father's pretending to be nuts, which made me angry, until I realized he couldn't control himself. But I really did think he was faking the whole thing. I thought the two of them together were putting on some show for the rest of us and it was supposed to do something for us. Then I began to look around and I said to myself, 'How come, Adrian, you're the only one in the family that seems to be taking things bad? You aren't the oldest or the youngest, but you sure are the only one not eating?' So then I figured, not only is it some kind of weird act, but I mean really weird, but I'm the only one who isn't onto it. You know what I mean? It's like the whole family was in on some secret except for me. Like they were testing me.

"So then I thought, if it *is* a test, what's it a test *for*? Has to be a test to see if I'm crazy? I mean, there's a mess of craziness going on in the house, I'm the queer one 'cause no one else seems much bothered by it, so that means I'm *it*. So I thought, okay, I got to either show them I'm not crazy, or I am. So I decided I might just as well show them I am, or make them think I am so they'll stop the test and tell me the big secret. So I stopped eating, at least they thought I did. You did too. But I was eating when nobody knew about it. At first anyway. Later, when I really got scared, I *did* stop eating. That's when I remembered that saying of my father's about how liars shouldn't eat. I really did think I was going to be crazy like him, except I was always afraid to think about him going crazy. I couldn't even say the words to myself. My father *isn't* crazy I'd tell myself. He's *not*, not, not, not, not crazy.

"If I was bad off then, I thought I'd go out the window when I came home one day from school and find out he wasn't there. I went past his room expecting him to be there like always, and nobody . . . The place was empty. You know the first thing I did? I went to all the windows to see if maybe he jumped out; I didn't know if that's what people like him did. That night I asked my mother; she said he was on a trip. You think I said anything? 'Where'd he go?' 'Well, we're not sure but he said he's for sure coming back.' One minute he can barely move his eyes, and he didn't know who I was before I gave up sticking my face up in front of him like a dummy. Then the next minute he's on a long trip. I thought he died. I didn't even think he was in a mental hospital. I thought he died and my mother was going on pretending. I figured she got his body out as fast as she could and made up her wonderful story about him taking a trip. Later that night my sister told me he was in the hospital in the northern part of the city or somewhere and now I could see how it was even more important that I didn't talk to anyone about it, not even to you. So I said okay, sure, fine. I can keep a secret, which I did, only I hit the first kid I saw the next morning at school. I told myself that's what I'm going to do. The first little kid, I'm going to pound him. If he survives he'll think I'm crazy, but I've already been working on that one.

"Then after that, I kept hitting kids. I couldn't control myself. I didn't want to even if I could have. I wanted to kill people really. They thought I was hurting them, but they should have felt what *I* felt. They were lucky I didn't kill them. I kept thinking of these guys you see on television who go *real* crazy and start shooting people for no reason. Jeez, once I thought those people were, like, from the moon. Now I could be one of them. Cops coming to shoot me like some wild animal after I'd killed a bunch of little kids or something. All I wanted to do was see my father. I told her take me there. 'Let me see him.' 'No. It's not for children.' 'I'm no child, Ma.' That's what I kept telling her. I'm no child. 'Stop calling me a child.' 'You're a child.' That's her standard answer: 'You're a child. Children don't have to know about this.' 'But *nobody* knows.' Oh man, we can scream at one another like two mental patients ourselves. I told her a couple of weeks ago, 'cause we really had a fight to beat all fights after I got suspended, I told her they locked up the wrong person. She hit me. She did. Foom, like I hit those kids! Maybe the reason I hit little kids is because she keeps treating me like *I* was a little kid. I don't know, maybe that doesn't make sense. Anyway I told her, 'You can hit me all you want, but they *did* lock up the wrong person. I'd rather have him here than you, even though he doesn't even know who we are half the time.' 'Yes, he does know,' she goes. She's always got to fight back; keep all the secrets going. I told her, 'Hey, man, I'm not going to break your big secret. Who'd I tell anyhow? No one's going to know, so don't worry.' 'You're not to talk about it,' that's all she says.

"I don't really know if I do or don't want to see my father in a mental hospital. It's hard for me to think about it. It's like everything else going on around here; I don't know anything. I always have to imagine it, and usually when you imagine things it's worse than they really are, so I don't know. I think I'd like to be there with him. Maybe he talks with people out there. Maybe if I was there he'd know he could trust me so he'd tell me something, like what he thinks about, *anything*! It's like another test: Prove you're crazy like him and he can speak his special language to you instead of turning his head away like he does. It's kind of like he doesn't want to know his own secret either. I'd start talking and he'd move away. I probably should have told him, 'Dad, you're crazy. Why not face it. You're crazy even if she won't let you think about it. You got to be thinking about *something*.' Maybe she took his mind away from him by making it all a big secret. Maybe when you keep that stuff in your mind, you go nuts. It happened with him, it sure looks to me like it could be happening with her too. I don't know.

"She should tell us what it's like in the hospital. She should tell us what he's like there. Does he sit in a chair and stare? Does he cry? Does he talk to anyone? For all I know they got him in a padded cell. Maybe he's in there this minute, banging his fists on the wall like those people do. He could kill himself in there and she'd probably tell us he decided to take a longer trip than he thought he would. I tell you, she's got this business of not letting anyone know; that man could die and she wouldn't say nothing. He could be dead now, but if she thought it wouldn't look good to someone to have him die, she'd say, 'Oh, I hear from him all the time, he's doing fine.' She'd be hearing from him, all right, from the damn grave. It'd be better to have him dead than have someone in the neighborhood know her husband's a mental patient.

"I'll give her one thing: She kept all her secrets. Nobody I know knows anything about it. They're probably asking questions but I've never heard anyone even come close to guessing where he is. Kids in school don't talk about their fathers, so she got everything she wanted. I guess my brother and sisters did too, 'cause I never heard them complain about anything. Everybody seems well adjusted around here except for Chico. W don't talk about it, none of us, so there I go again not knowing what anybody thinks. But I'm not going to stay with it like this. I'll give it a month 'til I reach my sixteenth birthday. I told her too. I told her, 'You got 'til I turn sixteen. If he ain't back here then, then I go to.' 'You got school,' she goes. 'You can take school and everybody in it,' I goes, 'and put it in the ocean. Put it in his mental hospital, why don't you!' She went to hit me, but I didn't let her touch me. I had to dance around the kitchen to get away from her, but I made out. 'Stick it in the loony bin. You get him here for my birthday, or I'm gone.' 'Go ahead,' she goes. 'Run away. Run away from all your problems.' '*My* problems? How come they're *my* problems?' I didn't even know 'til yesterday where he was and she calls them *my* problems. I'm telling you, she really is crazy.

"I know where he is. I called the place and found out how you get there. I told them my father's there and my mother's dead and I want to know how you get there. They told me. I'm going to visit him. I'll check the place out first. She can keep all her secrets but she can't lock me up. She's done enough to my mind. We're living in a family of psychological warfare. How do I know what she did to him all these years? You don't know what she said to him. I'm going to find him; I'll ask him. I'll go there every day and ask him. He'll tell me. He'll tell me all the secrets. It'll be like me saving him and him saving me."

Chico Adrian's announcement that he had learned the whereabouts of his father placed me in a difficult position. I couldn't very well visit Jack without Sally's permission. Nor could I raise the matter with her for that would be to break my word of confidentiality to Chico. So there I was, sucked into the family's web of secrets exactly as Chico had described it. When I asked Sally about Jack she told me the same story she had told her son: Jack was on a trip. I said nothing, but I made every facial gesture I knew, hoping to communicate my doubt. She saw my twitching but kept still. If I didn't buy her story that was my business. Before leaving I let her know, without equivocation, that I would continue to visit Chico. That was fine with her. Would she make special plans for his birthday? She wasn't certain. Would Jack be back from his trip (and my words here literally stunk with sarcasm)? She wasn't certain of this either.

I hated Sally Adrian in those moments, and I felt pity for her and compassion and anger and every other emotion her son felt as well. Her situation was wretched, and probably she had made it worse. Probably, too, she realized she had not improved things, but she was a proud woman and she would not back down. Stymied, I found no way to properly intervene. My attachment with the Adrians was precarious enough. Whenever I wondered about them, I would recall a friend saying to me, "If you can't force people to see a dentist when their teeth are falling out, how can you get a person to seek counsel for an overwhelming family predicament?"

Chico was my concern. In fact, he was gradually becoming an obsession. The thought of him committing suicide was not outlandish. He had seemed utterly inflexible in his ultimatum: A significant change by his sixteenth birthday or he would leave. His mother, I know, heard this firmness. "He's not a boy no more," she whispered, but she wasn't home the night of Chico's birthday. She left a beautifully wrapped package for him, but she had to be somewhere. I took

Chico, Ronald, and one of the girls, Patsy, for steaks, french fries, and hot apple pie. They seemed to enjoy the restaurant, although Chico wore a peculiar grin that evening.

Ronald told me a week later that Chico had carefully opened the present from his mother to see what it was, then wrapped it again so that she would think he had no interest in it. He didn't know that Ronald had spied on him, or that Ronald had told me about the unwrapping. The secrets pile had grown still higher. Then Chico threw out his own secret: He ran away, telling no one of his destination or plans. Ronald received a note in the mail but it held no clue to his whereabouts.

Learning of his disappearance, I telephoned the mental hospital. I was certain Chico would go there, if not immediately, then surely within a couple of weeks. Sally said he would return home when he cooled down. I tended to agree with her, but the doubt remained. The doubt grew when three months passed with no word from him. Ronald, who now had become my closest ally in the family, was deeply upset. All three children, for that matter, were convinced that Chico was dead. Interestingly, both daughters acted much like their mother when it came to befriending me. It was like they had convinced themselves never to change. From the beginning they had kept me at arm's length, and they would not waver from this position now, even though they expressed a need for me.

We contacted police, army recruitment offices, Chico's friends, but nothing turned up. Sally began going to church and taking the girls with her. Ronald refused on the grounds that it was hypocritical, and merely represented a way to ease her guilt. God knows how Jack Adrian was faring, although I did learn that he had been moved to another hospital—not that this signified improvement. Six months and still no word from Chico. Then eight, ten, and eleven months. No word, no hint, nothing. How tragically ironic that the final secret of this family was the whereabouts of their youngest son. Once again that same old motley collection of feelings welled up when I even thought of the Adrian name. Guilt, hate, anger, shame, fright, compassion, pity, helplessness. I was even growing angry at Chico, whose disappearance had the effect on all of us of a suicide. We were the survivors, consumed by "survivor feelings." I swore if I ever saw him again I would tell him his "trick" was unfair; his leaving was too much to ask of us. The mind hardly works in rational ways during such times.

Then one night, dinner time, a phone call. Our daughter answered. For me. Food in my mouth, irritation at being interrupted in my voice, "Hello." A strange voice, female, bad connection. Administrator at a mental hospital. Jack's first hospital. A boy had been admitted and she had found a card (from eleven months before) indicating I was to be called. My body turned ice cold; my palms began to perspire. Chico Adrian had committed himself.

The story is almost complete. Its ending, however, is far from satisfactory. Chico Adrian had travelled, seemingly, all over America. Looking for nothing, heading for nowhere, his mission merely was to keep moving. It went on this way for eight months, by which time he had reached the Pacific Coast, 3,000 miles from his home. He worked at this or that, stayed with people, did what he had to in order to keep going. As he told it, his spirits were good. While he felt like a fugitive and imagined himself to be the star of a television show, he was not without energy and confidence. Finally the coast, new friends, new life styles, new ideas and perspectives, some talk, although he kept his promise never to reveal his real name and address, and a great deal of alcohol and drugs. A weekly habit became a daily one, then a daily and nightly one. After a couple of months he was taking any drug anyone would offer. The cheaper they were, the more he liked them, no matter what their effect. Hospitalized on two occasions for overdosing, he was becoming known to certain medical authorities who tried their best to rehabilitate him, always without success. As one report on him noted, "He seems unable to limit, much less quell, his drug habit. He seems determined to become a full fledged mental patient with the rights and privileges thereof."

The observation was perfectly apt. While drugs "solved" some of Chico's problems, or at least reduced some of the pain, they had become a means by which he could accomplish his true goal: namely, to be placed in the same mental hospital as his father. It was, he later would admit, the only way he could "break into" the place and find out the truth of his father. Exhibiting a fair amount of ingenuity, he worked his way back across the country, and using drugs and alcohol to achieve his psychotic state, he managed to be admitted to the hospital where originally his father had been placed. He was not aware that Jack had been transferred nine months before. By this point, Chico's intentions had become painfully transparent. Upon being admitted to the hospital he gave his name as Jack Adrian, and presented his parents' home address and telephone number. He also said he was the father of four children, two boys and two girls, although one of the boys, Chico, had died from strangulation. Apparently the boy had divulged too many family secrets so his mother choked him to death!

The hospital admitting officers needed little more from the young man to confirm their diagnosis: "Paranoid schizophrenic, symptoms exacerbated by addiction to alcohol and hard drugs. He also reveals suicidal and homocidal tendencies." During his first several days in the hospital, Chico Adrian was placed in solitary confinement. This was done, it was said, "for his own good." At the end of a month he was able and willing to talk to me and a young social worker, who expressed willingness to work with him. Chico was quiet, sullen, recalcitrant, at first, but the social worker won him over with kindness. It was clear I would have to remove myself from the scene; I was too deeply associated with the past, the confusing, torturous, and evil past. I was also implicated in the secrets. I bowed out, just as Chico requested, leaving the door open for him to contact me at any time, for any reason. He shook hands when I left him at the hospital the last time. Moments before he had been laughing, somewhat ingenuously, over his "breaking in" escapades. It was utterly humorous to him to find that his father had been transferred. "How come you didn't say anything about that?" he asked me flatly.

"You didn't ask," I joked.

"Hey" he responded, and here his response was as sharp and alert as I had observed since his hospitalization, "I found out a long time ago you don't get nothing from asking. You can't even find out simple little things from your own mother. She kept me away from my father. She kept the truth out of my head. Now they got a whole lot of people wanting the truth out of my head. Why don't they ever ask me about all those people who shoved lies into my head in the first place? That's why I had to clean myself out. All those secrets everybody had, they were just air; air and shit. That's why I had to pump them out of my system. And find my father. I'm dedicated to it now. I'll find him. I'll track him down. There can't be all that many mental bins or graveyards in this country. I'll go from one to the other. I'll find him. Don't worry none, I'll let you know when I run across him. Him seeing me is going to cure him, you know. And me seeing him ain't going to do me no harm neither. I don't care what the hell my mother does about all this. She can float in the ocean for all I care. I haven't give up yet. They wrote I got suicidal tendencies. That's supposed to mean I want to kill myself. Can you imagine doctors being so wrong! I don't want to kill nobody. I wouldn't touch a fly. All I want is a little get together with some special people where we talk about the old days. How's that sound, the old days! A little get together, a little talk, and a secret pledge to have no more secrets. That ain't all that much, is it? You call that much? Wouldn't cost the state a penny!"

I couldn't keep myself from taking these almost parting words as a challenge to me. I chose to interpret the sentiment, moreover, in a sentimental manner: "Send me my mother and father," which is what I did. First his mother visited him, then his parents came together, for Jack was making sufficient progress, and finally, three months after my last conversation with Chico, Jack Adrian came alone to Ward 11-H to see his youngest son. A nurse described the meeting as the most moving scene he had ever witnessed. Whatever feelings both had about the other, and the past as well, they were concealed during the meeting when Sally was present. Alone, they wept and embraced and spoke for hours without respite. Jack Adrian, the nurse reported, spoke with animation, and his son smiled and laughed. And both men seemed younger and younger with each passing minute.

The substance of that first of many conversations between father and son is known only to them. It remains, until now, their secret.

7

I'm Going to Play with the Souls of Your Children

Raymond Herman hitched up his belt and spread his legs slightly as he stood on the gymnasium floor looking out at the boys running about in front of him. The noise in the gymnasium was deafening, hundreds of games and battles, it seemed, were taking place simultaneously. Yet Ray Herman seemed not to hear a whisper. After staring at the children, his eyes would move in space as if what he was about to say were written somewhere, written in the smells and sounds of the gymnasium where only he could read them.

Searching for the proper starting point, he smiled modestly, a schoolboy in that instant hunting desperately as time ran out for an answer to a complicated mathematics problem. Perhaps he wasn't alone in the gymnasium. Perhaps there were others watching him.

In the Porter Elementary School where Ray Herman has worked for the last six years as an administrator and part-time physical education instructor, they say that there are as many Ray Hermans as there are people willing to talk to him. Some report he is one of the kindest gentlemen they have ever known. Others claim he is the meanest, quick-tempered, and ill-mannered middle-aged ruffian they have ever had the displeasure of meeting. Some see him as tough and contentious; others as generous, giving, and a loyal friend. Ray Herman himself loves the myriad labels thrown at him. He will say straight out that the way to be a successful school administrator is not to let anybody know who you really are. Treat each person and each situation as the moment warrants, but let no one get close enough to sabotage your work.

"School's a high-powered intelligence game," he once told a group of people. "You got to keep an eye open for everything that happens. Teachers don't have to think this way, but there's not an administrator I know doesn't have to figure out ways to learn what's going on in his school. You set up your spies, you find out. That means you do a little strong-arming with some people and a little soft-talking with others.''

"And does that mean," someone asked him, "that you yourself are so many different people you don't even know who you really are?''

"I know me, baby," Ray shot back quickly. "I know me all I need to know. Don't you worry about that!''

The boys in the gymnasium were running laps before retiring to the locker room. Ray Herman barely saw them. He was scratching his head, careful not to mess his neatly combed pitch-black hair.

"All right, here it goes. I think man has made all sorts of fabulous inventions to help him. You know what I mean? Someone had to understand what fire could do for man, and the wheel, and all the rest. Busing's got to stack up as the number one error ever made, maybe in the history of mankind. Whoever designed the concept is a lunatic. Either that, or he's somebody very, very rich who never once put his kid on a bus. You take World War Two. Why'd we fight in World War Two? Because a madman was getting set to take over the world. The man had destroyed Poland, devastated it. Moved into Holland, sent millions of innocent people into prisons you wouldn't put a dog into, killed 'em. Killed women, killed babies. I mean, this was a madman. Either you got him or he'd eat you alive. Nobody could disagree with that. Jesus Christ, the people in France and England would have cut off their arms for us the day we won that war. Should we have been there? You bet your sweet you know what we should have been there.

"Vietnam War? Korean War? You can argue it any way you like, up one side, down the other. But you can't look back at these things. You look at them, both these wars, as they looked when they began, when we first got into them. And I say we should have been in both of 'em. Certainly we had a place, a commitment in Korea. You make promises to these countries, and you have to keep to them. More madmen trying to take over something that isn't theirs. That's what all these wars are about. Look at it this way. You got two kids, not children, grown-up kids. We'll make 'em fourteen, fifteen. Here they are, right in the middle of the gym, going at each other. They'd kill each other if someone didn't stop them. All right? Now, you think another kid that age is going to interfere? Not a chance. Doesn't have the strength, but more important, he doesn't have the smarts. He's too excited with the fight. He's pulling for one of the guys maybe, or maybe he's hoping someone will get hurt. He doesn't even know the kids who are fighting but he wants someone hurt. It happens. So now you're me or some teacher, an adult. You interfere? Fast as you can. That's Korea and Vietnam as I see it.''

Ray Herman had begun walking through the large double door. The boys, save for a few stragglers, had disappeared into the locker room at the other end of the gymnasium. He fixed his tie and buttoned the middle button of his brown tweed suit jacket. No matter what anyone said about Ray Herman's personality, everyone agreed he looked at least ten years younger than his age. No one questioned his manners, moreover. He rose from his chair in the presence of a woman, he never passed through a door without holding it for anyone with whom he happened to be chatting. It was the same with those who worked for him as with those he did not know. His manners were impeccable; his colleagues appreciated this quality in him.

"All those wars," Ray Herman was saying as he headed toward his second floor office," were caused by people bullying people. People who hadn't the singlest right in the world to force other people to do things against their will. That's busing in a nutshell. It's got nothing to do with racial prejudice. Believe me, I know. I couldn't care less what Negroes do with their children. They want to send them to their schools, ship them off to our schools, I couldn't care less. But *telling* people, *ordering* them, you gotta go here or there, seems to me that's exactly what the whole damn set of wars we've been fighting for fifty years is all about. Nobody can make such a policy. They may *think* they can, but no one has that kind of power!

"Are there prejudiced people in this school? I'd have to say yes, there are. I could name them if I had to. I know people in this school who can't stand the fact they have to teach Negro children. You can hate these people if you want, but I prefer to feel sorry for them. All they're doing is living with the feelings and attitudes their parents gave them. They're not bad people, they just haven't grown up. In many ways, I'll admit it, they really aren't a helluva lot more mature than the children they teach. It's a fact. We had an assistant principal in this school for twenty years before I came. Actually we overlapped the first year I was hired. You want to talk about mean, here was a guy who just told the Negro kids, 'I don't care a damn how much you guys want to play on a basketball team. Long as I'm here there won't be a Negro on any team.' He told 'em this right out. I heard him one time. I thought I'd fall over. Kids came to me to help them. Jesus, I had parents screaming in my office. 'It's against the law, it's against the law,' they were yelling. It was a goddam zoo here then. Third week in this new job and I'll bet I had every parent of every Negro kid in the whole school pushing and shoving in my office. There was nothing I could do. That guy Kierney, Harry Kierney was his name, the late, great Harry Kierney, he couldn't be budged. He had the power. I'd have spoken up against him, I'd have been not only out of this school, I'd have been out of the *system*. So I told these parents, I'll do what I can, but I knew there wasn't a thing I could do. And that old weasel was good to his word too. There wasn't a Negro boy on a single school team. Not one. You talk about outbursts, I thought those kids would burn down the school. I'll tell you something else. I wouldn't have blamed them. They were being deprived. No doubt about it. They were being screwed to the wall. If it had happened to me, I'd have been tempted to do away with that weasel. I might have done anything to stop him.''

Ray Herman lowered himself into his huge leather-backed desk chair that seemed to moan under the weight of his body. The walls of the old office were lined with diplomas, charts, tables depicting costs, students' grades, and attendance records. Of his many obligations, his prime concern was daily attendance. He had made a pledge when he began the job that at any minute of any day he would know exactly how many children were out of school and why. It had become a mission, a passion really, this interest in absent children. A child's tardiness might upset him slightly, but to know that children were missing from school for long periods of time deeply annoyed him. He often said that one of his great quarrels with busing was that students were kept out of school and refused to go. The numbers on his attendance chart soared, and rather than muster the strength it took to account for all the absences, he would fall into a state of sadness. Some people in the school claimed that Ray Herman actually grew depressed when large numbers of students were absent. It was strange, almost frightening to see him during these times. They wondered about him, sensing a rage behind the sadness, an anger directed at someone that only he knew.

The man many students called "Tiger Boy" because he would prowl quietly about the rooms of the enormous school checking up on people and stalking missing children, was well aware of his attitudes about attendance and the feelings evoked in him by low attendance figures.

"No, you don't want to blame this anti-busing attitude on people being prejudiced. Harry Kierney was a prejudiced man. There was no way else you could see that man. He hated them. Show him black skin and he'd damn near go into some kind of fit. But that's not what gets most people about the busing. It isn't the mixing of the kids, it's the pushing people around. Telling a man, I don't care that you've spent your life working to make the money to live in this one small block of one small community in the middle of this city. I don't care that you want to live near the people you grew up with and your parents and maybe grandparents grew up with. I don't care that you want to keep your children with their own kind so they can see how important it is for them to learn about their own kind, the history of their people *and* their neighborhood. I'm going to bus your kids God only knows where. Don't worry, I got tests here that say it won't hurt them any. I don't care that you Irish got feelings about your neighborhood, or you Italians or you Germans or you Portugese. That don't mean nothing to me. I'm going to move your children all over hell and gone just so I can mix up the schools a little bit. That's what it's all about. That's the objection people raise to busing. It isn't constitutional, hasn't been from the day these people, whoever the hell they are, put it in.

"What you're doing with busing is saying to people, 'I'm breaking up your family. You got all these connections with the people you live with, your ancestors, people who made you what you are? Well, I'm going to do something that will break your backs. Play with your pocket book? Nope, I ain't going to touch your money. Mess with your job? Nope, I couldn't care less what you're doing. Mess with your stores, your churches? I ain't going to touch a building any-where. You know what I'm going to do? I'm going to play with the souls of your children. I'm going to take the most important people to you and I'm going to mess with their minds. I'm going to bus 'em all over this goddam city so they won't even know where they're going half the time, or who their new friends are, or their old friends for that matter.' That's what these boys who practice busing are saying to these white families. They are telling these families, all right, you can do all the protesting and bellyaching you want, but we'll take your kid out of your house and truck 'em all over hell, even if we have to do it over your dead bodies. And they would too.

"These people get an idea in their mind that innocent kids have to be bussed, there isn't a soul in the world going to stop them. Not even the President. I honestly can't blame these families for keeping their children out of school. They should never let themselves be pushed around like this. Makes my job harder, of course, having to count the missing ones and go looking for them, but I can't blame these parents. I'll tell you something, in general principle now, I think it's more important for these families to keep their children *out* of school than it is to let them come right now. You have to make a start on principles. You have to say to people, 'I won't do it!' You can't shove me around any more. I won't have it. It's better for these classrooms to go empty, really, all of them, than have these people beaten down by people who couldn't give a damn about them. Believe me, I know the feeling. I know the feeling of having someone push you down until you're practically owned by them, and watching them drive off in their rich man's cars, telling you they care about your life when all they're worried about is getting what they want. They don't care about you or me, those people. Believe me, I know all about them."

Ray Herman turns his head slowly from side to side as though watching the path of a ball being tossed back and forth. There is pain in his body that shows on his face. He is a man eager for retaliation, revenge, but the movement of his head and the surprising calmness in his body says that there will never be revenge for the scene he now imagines.

The coal mining towns in Pennsylvania have struggled in the same ways and survived the same circumstances as the mining towns in West Virginia, only the ones in Pennsylvania rarely receive national attention. When catastrophe hits them, the newspaper people come running and the usual cries are heard about the lack of mine safety. But the rest of the time—and the years are long in these towns—no one visits, no one comes to hear about or witness the everyday world of the families who have been here, it seems, forever.

As a small boy, Ray Herman, whom the neighbor children always called Ray-Ray, used to wait anxiously for school to be over so he could run to the entrance to the mines and watch the men, dirty, grimy, coughing, come out of the giant tunnels and elevators. The rule of the mine was that no one as young as Ray-Ray was allowed anywhere near the mine entrances. Still the ritual of running from school to the entrance and seeing his father and his father's three brothers ascend from the pits each day gave him almost as much pleasure as actually descending into the underground world with the men. "When I get big like Daddy and Uncle Teddy and Uncle Billy and Uncle Monty," he would tell his mother, "I'm going to work down there too."

Lorraine Herman would shrug. If she had to, she would blow up the mine before permitting her son to work down there. Her grandfather had started mining when he was eleven years old, her father when he was fifteen. Her husband, John Herman, known to everyone as Jock, was sent away from home in order to finish high school. He lived with relatives near Pittsburgh who urged him to think hard about going to college. As he laughingly told everyone years later, that's exactly what he did. He thought hard about college. The day after graduating from high school, where his grades had been good and where he had performed marvelously as a football player and trackman, he returned to the place of his birth and entered the same mining company that employed his father. One week after graduating he was working side by side with his father, a man approaching fifty-five.

Jock Herman saw his father die on the old green flowered sofa in the small row house on Ligonier Road. The man was coughing up blood for five weeks before his wife could get a doctor to examine him. A representative of the mine had stopped in several times to check on him, but it was five weeks before a doctor came. When he did, there was nothing he could do but suggest to Mrs. Herman and Jock that they bring the old man into the hospital. "I'd rather have him die in his own home," Mrs. Herman had responded. "The man grew up in this town, lived his entire adult life in this house, that's where he wants to be now."

"You're making a mistake," the doctor had said respectfully. But young Jock could hear in the man's voice that he understood. His father was a proud man, proud of his physical strength, proud of the way he had maintained himself over the last thirty-five years. He enjoyed flexing his large forearms and gripping things tightly with his giant hands. Jock could never think about his father without imagining the strong hands, the long well-shaped fingers, and the rich color of the fingernails.

"You're making a mistake," the doctor had repeated as he opened the front door to the Herman's home.

"Hell she is." It was John Herman himself, standing weakly, then heaving his thin body against the wooden door jamb. His cheeks were sunken in, and his hair, always so finely black, looked damp. The signs of his former strength were there, but his son could see the man was dying. Please don't let him die standing there with the doctor here, young John said to himself. "Hell she is," his father was saying over and over again, barely able to get the words out before being stricken by a paroxysm of coughing, his body lurching as if the final remains of his shredded lungs had just been expelled.

The doctor merely nodded and left, but he, like Jock, had seen death in John Herman's eyes. There was no need to take the old man to the hospital. The Mrs. had been right. Jock helped his father to his bed in the small alcove adjoining the front room but the man signaled that he preferred to lie down on the couch just as his wife had said. Jock held his father around the chest, frightened by his thinness. John Herman lay on the couch perfectly still, except for the fits of coughing which always caused a small amount of blood to come from his mouth. For two days he remained there. The room smelled of his feces and urine. "It's the stink of death," Jock's mother whispered, apologizing to friends who came to her door. "You live your life with the stink of the mines. Every day the same sights, the same smells, the stink of the mines. They give you life all right, if you call that measly sum of money life. Then the stink of death comes and it's all over for your man." The neighbors and friends since childhood nodded. How deeply they felt her words, and how much they honored her clear-eyed resignation and her understanding of what it was all about.

Jock Herman was asleep in a chair when his father died. His mother woke him to say that the Lord had taken the man they loved away. "I don't want you to cry now," she told her son, the only one of her four children still living in the house on Ligonier Road. "There'll be plenty of time for crying. That's the minister's business. I want only one thing for you now, right in this moment when your father's body is still warm from the bits of life he had while he was with us. You promise me that your children will never once in their lives see the insides of those mine pits. Never once. This must end. No one dies in this country at such ages. Men beaten at the age of thirty and thirty-five from work conditions not fit for cattle and dogs. And all these men running around here at election time telling us this and that and making promises not one of them intends keeping. They haven't fooled me for forty years. Their type only knows one way of talking, and that's lying."

Jock Herman promised his mother that he would be the last in the family to work the mines. Years later, the promise proved especially difficult for his children, particularly Ray-Ray and James, because as the only boys, it was frustrating to tell their friends that their father refused to hear of their desire to work in the mines with him, as he had worked with Big John, their grandfather whom they had never known. Ray-Ray told himself that maybe if he ran to meet his father and his uncles every day after school, it might change his father's mind. The technique had worked in the past. Jock would refuse his sons something, but they would beg and nag him until he broke down and gave in to them. Lorraine disliked seeing Jock so easy with the boys. She said that a child had to understand the meaning of the word "no," but Jock would argue that if parents had something, why not give it to their children. "The girls are better-mannered," Lorraine would say. "Girls are supposed to be," Jock would come back, running his large hands through James's or Ray-Ray's long straight hair. Then the boys would run off, happy that of all the fathers in the world, even the rich ones, they had Jock as their dad.

Occasionally Ray-Ray waited around outside the kitchen to hear what his mother might say after he and James had left. But it wasn't his mother who spoke when the boys, presumably, were out of hearing distance; it was his father.

"I'm not going to live that long anyway," Jock would say. "How long you think it's going to be before the whole business kills me off? If it isn't the lungs, it will be a disaster. It's got to be something. All these strong bodies, like my father's, they can't hold up more than a few years against it. Nothing's going to change. Nothing's changed and nothing will. They come in their cars, make their foolish inspections, and leave. The senators, the big men, all of them. My mother was right about them. You see any changes that will make any of it better for us? There's not a hope. Tomorrow, forty or sixty-eight could come down, and don't think for a minute the timber they got down there is worth a nickel. Or the gases may leak, or a fire or a mechanical failure. We'd all go. Like that." Ray-Ray would hear his father's broad hand smack down on the wiggly rough-top table where the six of them ate breakfast.

"Mine's no stronger than this table. Any minute it goes. It will go, too, 'cause the big men of this country make rules and set down laws and tell little people like us what to do, where to go to work every morning, how to raise our children. They wouldn't have this sort of living for nothing. There isn't one of those people who owns anything that would trade places with us. Not one of them. I know. I know them now the same way my mother knew them. Same way my father and your father knew them, only *they* knew they had to keep their mouths shut. When those gates open in the morning and close in the afternoon, you better be there. When they call your name, you better just be standing there. That's what those bosses talk about with us. Safety, health, a little bit of money, as though it would kill them, not a word of honesty comes from them. Just be there when they call your name, and for God's sake, don't get sick too soon or the insurance benefits won't even pay your woman enough to eat for a year. So you tell me what it's worth."

"We've talked about this before," Ray-Ray would hear his mother say, knowing she couldn't appease her husband. "We both know it. Why carry on with the same words?" Ray-Ray could hear them moving about in the kitchen which always seemed cold, even in the autumn before the weather changed. It seemed dusty, too, no matter how often his mother cleaned, which was once a day. There was no way to keep anything clean. The air was filled with the dust, the evil sprinkle as his grandmother called it, the devil's dirt. The children said it never bothered them, they never knew it was there. But their parents said when you got older you never got used to it.

"It was like being blind," Lorraine had told Ray-Ray and his sister Judith. "You know you can't see. You may not think about it, but when you go to see, you can't. It's the same with the dirt. When you go to breathe deeply, you can't do it. It's killing us off slowly.''

"Even the children?'' Judith had asked.

"Even the children,'' Lorraine had nodded. "The bosses and owners could make it better for all of us, but they never will.'' The children had looked at each other, not fully understanding their mother, but certainly aware of what her phrase "even the children" meant.

No matter how the discussions started, Ray-Ray, either standing in the kitchen with his parents or overhearing them, they invariably ended the same way, with his father's speech:

"No one's telling my children how to live their lives. If there're other children around here who want to do what their fathers do, that's fine, but not these boys. They're not going to work with, they're not going to have their souls owned by people who'd sell them out cheap. Don't let anyone fool you, Lorraine. The ones I watch the closest are the ones who used to work in there with us. Going about saying how they'll protect us when they get the chance. They'd sell their mothers off too, like all those other ones. Just give them the chance. Everybody wants to be out of here. Any chance that comes along they'll grab on to it. There aren't those chances for us, so I'm telling you when the time is right, you're taking those kids out of here. With me or without. You cannot keep doing the things your grandparents and great grandparents set up for you to do. Someone has to say, 'Stop.' My sons won't follow me.''

Jock Herman died at the age of thirty-eight, when Ray-Ray was eleven years old. A gas leak in the mine, an explosion, a mistake, the reason for his death was never determined. The family went to the main office of the mine where Jock Herman and the other miners, one of whom looked at first to be his brother but wasn't, were brought up. Lorraine Herman barely cried. It seemed as though she knew this day was coming. For months prior to the accident, Jock Herman had been depressed. He had talked about ending his life, and not caring if he got caught some night a million feet deep in the earth.

The bodies of the men lay on the floor, on their backs, their faces and hands filthy with coal dust. Ray-Ray went with his mother and his oldest sister Helen. The children looked at their father who appeared to be sleeping. A man went to Ray-Ray shaking his head slowly. He was well-dressed and his face and hands were clean. He whispered, "The niggers of the earth. Rotten mine niggers.'' Later that evening, as he lay in bed crying, Ray-Ray heard his mother moving busily about the house. She was already packing. The day after the funeral, she moved the children to her sister's home in Wheeling, West Virginia.

Ray Herman did not return to the town of his birth until he was twenty-eight years old. Married and the father of three children, his oldest boy having been named John after his father and grandfather, he had taken his family on a vacation to eastern Pennsylvania. They had toured Pennsylvania Dutch country for several days when suddenly he was overcome with a desire to visit his father's grave. He hunted in the town on a Saturday morning for people he thought he remembered, but although store owners knew the names, no one could be located. Ray visited with his Uncle Ben, one of the men who had worked with his father, now in his early sixties and in surprisingly good health. Then he went to the small cemetery on the knoll just west of town. From the top of the knoll he could see the hills and mountains, and the road leading to the main entrance of the mine where his father had died. He watched cars pass on the road and found himself trembling with fright and rage. He feared that he might faint at the sight of the grave, or break down and cry. He recalled the faces of the owners who attended his father's funeral and searched his memory trying to remember how his mother had received them. They were enemies of his family, yet it seemed his mother was willing to be comforted by them. Perhaps they had given her money.

The grave was smaller than he had remembered, a low stone with his father's name and the dates of his birth and death, overrun with wild flowers and a greenish moss on which slugs attached themselves. Ray could only look down at the bit of land, so undistinguished and plain, and wonder why he had come. He was unaware of the tears until he saw them falling on the ground near his feet.

For two hours, Ray Herman, his sleeves rolled up and his shoes muddy with the brown dirt, ripped away the weeds and moss that grew on his father's and grandparents' graves. Then he went to the village, bought small flowering plants and vegetable seeds, and returned to the grave sites. There, until the light was so poor he could barely see, he planted the flowers and the seeds, telling himself that it would now be lovely, and in the Spring there would be food for his father to eat. The greens near the graves, he whispered, would purify the air. He was amused by his child-like reasoning, but pleased that he had made the trip. As he walked away from the graves for the last time, his hands and arms dirty from the planting, he heard the words of the well-dressed man with the clean finger-nails who had whispered to him the afternoon the workers had brought his father's body up from the mine: "Rotten mine niggers." They did look like niggers, too, he thought, the filth of their skin matching the filth of their clothes. He asked himself, how could the owners let it come to this?

"There's a lot of my childhood tied up in this busing thing, I'll tell you," Ray Herman was saying as he glanced at the papers covering his large metal desk. "I can't help but think of all the people in the world being bullied, pushed around. I'll tell you now the same words I heard my father tell my mother. Fact, I can't even think about busing without hearing his voice, though I barely remember the sound of it. I only have one photograph of him. Can you imagine after all these years that people would live like they did and not have more than one photograph of themselves? I don't know that the man ever had an identification card with his picture on it other than the one he carried for the mine. But he said it all. Some people are born to work in the mines, do the rotten jobs, die young. Other people are born to make sure that those people keep doing those rotten jobs and die young.

"Everybody's up in arms about busing. They got a right to be. But then you read how these other people, the so-called intelligent members of the city, are so surprised or outraged by the protest. The rich Irish look down at the poor Irish, the rich Italians look down at the poor Italians. It's always the same. These well-to-do people, living out there in their comfortable suburban homes, what they're really saying is they're surprised that all these working-class types are putting up such a protest. They're angry with the protestors, they see these people as standing in their way.

"It's exactly like the miners' union types taking on the owners. Oh, the owners will act polite in front of the public and make these nice statements how it's important to sit down at the negotiating table and talk out the differences. But deep down they're thinking, what's come over you people that you think you have the right to argue with us on these matters. Our business is to make the decisions; your business is to accept whatever the hell we decide. I can see these rich people, some of them who grew up in the same areas where the families now are being asked to bus their children, saying, 'What in the name of the Lord are these people causing all this trouble about? In the first place, they aren't smart enough to come up with any good arguments to busing, and in the second place, it's their obligation in society to keep their tiny little mouths shut and follow orders!'

"I see school buses rolling in, I see these kids, black and white coming into this school, any school really, doesn't make a difference, I tell myself, here come the little miners. Here come the little miners thinking life's really going to be different for them now. The only mistake my father made was not to let me and Jimmy hear those conversations he had with my mother. I was only five or six, but they should have let us listen. What he said was more important than anything I ever learned in college or graduate school. That man knew wisdom because he lived it. He lived those experiences on the earth and so far beneath it, it would scare those judges out of their minds to go down there where he went every day to earn his living. He knew damn well what slavery was all about because he was a slave himself. You know in the south a lot of the slaves got paid? Did you know that? A lot of them got money for the work they did. Miners got paid. Some of them don't do all that badly, actually, if they can survive long enough where they've accumulated enough years. Lots of people working in this country who get paid are still slaves. Don't you make a mistake about it. But don't you think they like what they do or that they don't go home at night and tell their wives the same things my father told my mother. It's amazing that she was willing to listen to the same speech as often as she did.

"Well, busing's now a part of that speech. He didn't know a thing about it, of course, but the speech fits. Absent owners pushing hard working people around, people who never complained. I grew up knowing that. My parents used to tell us how we had to act if we met these rich people. 'Got to be polite, make them think we're grateful,' my mother used to say. I'm sure he said the same thing, but I honestly can't remember my father telling us we had to act nice in front of them. Jesus, he must have hated them. The same way these parents who are causing all the fuss hate the people who are telling them how to live their lives now.

"When my father looked around him he saw the same thing, the same world, his father saw. He saw the same houses, the same roads, same stores, same people, same jobs. Day after day, year after year, nothing changed. There wasn't anything that *could* change. It had to be the same. But nobody was telling him what to do with anyone in his family, directly that is. It was understood how he'd lead his life, of course, but no one legislated about his children. If he had a way of getting out, he got out. Goodbye. But this busing thing, it says this is what you *have* to do with your *children*. Now I mean, that has to take the cake as being the most unfair, illegitimate law that ever came over the mountain. It's like these owners saying, not only do the men go down, they *have* to, don't you see. And they would have passed that kind of legislation too if they thought it was in their best interest to do it. I know them. They'd have crushed anyone who got in their way. You know what they would have done if people had protested their rulings, they'd have taken them out and beaten them to a half-living pulp. Don't kid yourself. You're supposed to have a right to assembly in this country? You're supposed to be protected when you protest? They never would have allowed it. Those miner families were imprisoned. Go and look at their houses. See how they lived, how they're living today. Go see them. They're nothing but prisoners. And the people being bused are even in worse shape for one important reason. They're being led to believe they're free. But the government has taken a bunch of hostages: their children. The children, all of them, they're just hostages. The parents are told they're free, free to live where they want and work where they want and think what they want and worship where they want. But the children are hostages. You tell me where you're going to find a man or woman thinking they're free and happy when someone in the government or in a law court has their children tied up! Tied up. I mean it.

"Busing's a sham, my friend, one of the biggest swindles this country's ever seen. I'll tell you something else. These Negro families who think they're benefiting from it, I feel sorry for them. I swear to God, I feel just as sorry for them as I do for the white families. They're being lied to and tricked. The country's not doing a damn thing for them. You see the way they live, half of them. You believe the government would allow people to live in half those projects the government paid for itself? Someone got it in his mind that segregated schools were bad. So they integrate them and now nobody can find any way to prove that black children or white children are doing any better, or any worse for that matter, from all this disruption and confusion and nonsense. You go talk to the black families, really get in there and talk to them like I do, they'll tell you the same thing. You know what busing does? It takes a whole lot of people for a ride. It's a tease, a pretty expensive one, but it's a tease, that's all it is. It's doing no good at all and one helluva lot of harm. To both sides, too. Believe me.

"I had a mother in here not three days ago. 'Mr. Herman,' she says, and she's practically crying as she's talking to me, 'You got to help us switch schools.' That's what she's coming to me for. Three days ago. Right in the middle of the term. Her life's too disrupted. That kid of hers has to go God only knows how long in a bus, fifty minutes maybe, for no good reason, and she's sitting home all day worrying about what's happening to him. She doesn't even think about whether he's learning anything coming all the way over here. You know what I told her? 'There's not a thing in the world I can do.' Officially, I follow the rules. Rules say if your child is supposed to be bused, then he gets bused. If I had anything to say about all this, I'd have put an end to this idiocy a long time ago, certainly before it got this far. But I told her, if she can get the rules changed so there's no more busing, I'd be the happiest man in the world to obey those laws. And she'd be a helluva lot happier too. Believe me. Everybody would be happier, except the big people, of course. They're only happy when the money rolls in and their cute little ideas that help no one but themselves get put into action and everyone obeys them.''

Ray Herman was standing up near the door to his office where the large attendance charts were taped to the wall. His weight shifted from one side to the other and he pushed his hands against the papers to hold them flat. He screwed up his face, making calculations of some sort, trying to conjure up, it seemed, the faces of the absent ones. Today's list appeared particularly long. He rubbed his cheek against the grain of his whiskers making a gentle crackling sound. He didn't seem particularly perturbed by the large number of students he would attempt to contact, but it did seem that he might have been looking beyond the list to others no longer counted in the attendance rolls.

Without turning away from his work, and speaking to the large paper charts, he said: "Funny, everybody called me Ray-Ray when I was a kid except my father. He had nicknames for me, of course. All fathers do that. Tiger, Buster, Big Fellow. But usually he just called me Ray, or son. I could never remember what the hell I called him until that time I visited the grave. It came to me when I was working there, trying to clean the place up a little. I kind of heard myself say 'Daddy.' Sounds weird, doesn't it, a grown man calling his father 'Daddy.' But I never spoke to him much as a little boy. Hell, he died before he ever reached the age of a grown man. I mean, he was young when he died.''

Ray Herman turned finally and rubbed his hands together as though warming them. He shook his head in that way that says what follows is sarcasm. "My father, young when he died. You could just as well say young when they killed him, along with those other two men. That's what people with power do. They don't just make decisions that affect your life, or the lives of your children. They kill when they see fit, even if they do it so indirectly nobody recognizes what they're doing and when they're doing it. The real leaders in a country lead you into life. The powerful owners, they lead you into death. Believe me, I know. They lead you to the brink, in a mine shaft, maybe even on a school bus. If you don't die from what they do, you can count yourself as one of the lucky ones. But don't go celebrating the fact that you're still alive 'cause there's always your mother and father to wonder about, and there's always your children. There's always the children.''

8

A Mother's Son

Menachim Kanter was a man seemingly consumed by the sense of himself as a consummate failure. One saw it in his style and tone, in the expression of anger, his abiding feeling of shame. A thin man, though not frail, with a receding hairline and long thin fingers which made one believe he rarely worked with his hands, Menachim Kanter carried a sadness about him that was always left uncovered. In conversation he would jump quickly to the theme of personal failure and the sense of shame that failure brings to Jewish people, although, he would have said, to Jewish men. Surely he maintained a great respect for women, and a deep regard and love for his wife, but he made it clear again and again that men can fail in ways that women cannot. When a man fails, it destroys generations of families. It damages the expectations of parents, ruins opportunities for children, and makes life miserable for everyone. Women just don't have this burden, Menachim would say softly.

For Menachim Kanter, the strain of failure and the brooding unhappiness were exacerbated by the death of his mother in a German death camp. He barely remembered her, although her letters and photographs were brought to the United States when his father immigrated. While German was spoken in the house when he was a child, Menachim no longer could converse in the language, recalling only phrases and occasional words. When his Uncle Yankel spoke to him in German, he would nod, but he would understand very little. He remembered fragments of the trip to America, an argument at a Dutch custom's office over the authenticity of passports. But many of his recollections in fact are recollections of stories rather than remembrances of actual events. There was much uncertainty in his mind about the details of his escape from Germany when he was four; the homes in which he and his father, Morris, hid out; the people who fled with them. He remembered a woman who wore black dresses and insisted he call her "Aunt." She cared for him and a number of other children in a nursery. There was a toy train and a stuffed giraffe there that he believed were his, but when he left the nursery he was not allowed to take the toys. Because of this, he concluded that the woman must have been mean, and only pretended to be kind.

Morris Kanter and his brother Yankel remember the young Menachim as a lively, spirited boy, who, when he first arrived in America, seemed to like Hebrew School and eating potato chips more than anything else in the world. A package of potato chips in one hand, Yankel said once, the hagada in the other, and Menachim was utterly delighted. Menachim remembered nothing about the potato chips. He recalled Hebrew School as boring, but at least the building was warm, and the other boys were decent and hard working. He remembered, too, asking his father whether his mother had learned Hebrew. Morris answered emphatically, "Yes." In the orthodox community in which she was raised, Anna Kanter did not attend Hebrew School, but her father made certain she and her two sisters learned to read and write the language. So, Menachim asked, "If my mother learned it and she was killed, why should I learn it?" He no longer remembered his father's reply.

Nor did he remember the nights as a small child when he was unable to sleep and his father and other people who lived in his house tried to comfort him. He would tell them he was having bad dreams and was afraid to sleep because he knew the dreams would return. They let him play and sleep wherever he wished, but the nightly terrors persisted. Then, suddenly, when he was seven, they stopped. Menachim had heard of this behavior, but it always seemed that the events referred to another person.

Never one to like school, Menachim nonetheless was a good, if not extraordinary, student. He told himself that he could become outstanding if he worked hard. Someday, he promised himself, he would get himself to work hard, but that someday never came. Again and again he heard that education provided the one chance for him to make something of his life; the idea was beaten into his brain. Love of knowledge, the fun of playing with ideas or numbers was never discussed. Moreover, there was no one in the world to give him anything; whatever was to be earned would be earned by him.

Morris Kanter ran a small stationery business. He had been fortunate enough to raise a little money to start his business downtown where the demand for his goods would be highest. One year after the store opened, two office buildings went into construction, and Morris rejoiced at the thought of the increased business. But his expectations were never met. Business did improve with the erection of the buildings, but taxes and rent also increased, as did the price of paper goods.

Menachim remembered his father working every day. It was eight o'clock, usually, by the time his father arrived home, weak and exhausted. Morris Kanter was never a well man. The doctors worried about his periodic fainting spells and his constant fatigue, but could determine no illness. Occasionally, on Sundays, Menachim would spend time with his father, but mainly Morris needed to rest. When he found the energy, he preferred to pursue his great passion—checkers. If Menachim had one memory of childhood, it was going with his father to the tea house on Bancroft Street and watching his father play checkers. In the first hour or so, Menachim was intrigued by the game, but after that, he became bored and irritable. He played with the children of the other men, but they never became his friends. Sunday was checkers, Friday nights, when Morris wasn't tired, they went to schul. During the kadish Morris looked weepy, Menachim fought off feelings of sadness and boredom. Going to school made him want to speak to his father, but he could never get clear in his own mind what he would say if ever they found the proper moment for conversation.

If one word described Menachim Kanter's childhood, the word was *cold*. There were, of course, many nights in the small apartment when he could not get warm, even under four blankets. His left foot was always colder than the right. His nose ran and he breathed with difficulty. Coldness, however, also reflected his loneliness, and the hours he spent alone, making model planes, listening to the radio, watching the women work in the kitchen or clean around the house. He could watch people work for hours. Plumbers, painters, scrub women—he was fascinated by their movements. When noise outside announced the arrival of workmen. Menachim would dash out and stand in the cold, shivering, enchanted by the work. No one seemed to understand this fascination, although both his father and his Uncle Yankel worried that perhaps Menachim seemed excessively interested in manual labor. Menachim remembered their concern. He wouldn't have dared admit to wanting to become a plumber or carpenter. "So, what *do* you want to become?" Yankel would ask him. "I'm thinking," the boy would reply. "I'm thinking." He proferred that same answer when he was ten, on the night of his bar mitzvah, and still again when he was sixteen.

By the year of Menachim's bar mitzvah, Morris Kanter had become a sickly man who spent most of his time in bed. His business sold, he quickly expended his savings on medical bills, the little money he gave regularly to Yankel, an amount no one ever spoke about, and the expenses incurred by his son and the women who worked around the house. Although he received support from the state, there was never enough money. By the time Menachim was sixteen, his father, still only in his early fifties, was a gravely ill man. He was also a depressed man who possessed neither the physical nor psychic energy to seek new employment. For a while he did work in a stationery shop owned by Erwin and Jack Hayman, brothers whom Morris had once felt to be his strongest competitor. The Haymans had done extremely well. Opening a small shop about the same time as Morris Kanter opened his, they soon had expanded into the wholesale as well as retail end of the business.

The Haymans were delighted to have Morris working for them. Their father Aaron was one of the men with whom Morris played checkers. In his seventies, Aaron Hayman was known as the finest checker player in the neighborhood. Indeed, he loved checkers so much that he remained in the neighborhood only to be close to the tea house. Morris, in turn, was content to work for the Haymans, even though he felt like a charity case. "The Haymans need me," he told Menachim, "like a hole in *both* their heads. Their father told them, give the bum a job, so they gave me a job. Their father saves them money by living in the old neighborhood, so they got a little money kicking around. So they give it to me. That's what you call success, making it on your own. Maybe they don't like the idea of a refugee doing badly in a system of free enterprise. But Menachim, you know what I've learned—I've learned you don't question anybody, especially when they want to give you something. You don't say, 'I don't need a handout, it makes me feel small,' like a little boy taking all this generosity from people who once were almost like your enemies. You say, 'Thank you very much, I'll take whatever it is you want to give me. A job? Wonderful. When do I start?' You don't even ask, 'How much do I make?' Because one lousy question and they call you ungrateful, and before you know it, they take all the offers away.

"But *you*, Menachim, you won't be in this position. You'll tell them, 'A nice offer, a very nice offer. Tell me, what's the salary, what's the gimmicks.' And when you leave them, you won't tell them anything. You'll say, 'Let me think it over.' You keep them guessing so they know you have a brain for business, and you won't settle for the first thing that comes along. Most important in business, you never let the other person know you are desperate. They must always think your market is gigantic. If they don't give you the job you want, you have a list of offers long as your arm. You need them as much as you need your own eyes, but you have to make them think you can go somewhere else. Once they know you're in their grip, the price comes down and their *respect* for you goes with it. And when the price *and* the respect come down, you find yourself in the position I'm in with Aaron Hayman and his sons. They tell me ten cents an hour, I take it. And they know it. They're not dumb, these people. Oh no, they are very intelligent. So you have to be more intelligent than they are, all the time."

Menachim was sixteen when he heard these words, although he heard similar messages all his life. No matter what the words were, Morris' message to his son was always the same: Don't end up like me. Publicly he proclaimed himself to be the world's number one failure. Even his brother Yankel, who never worked, was more successful at whatever he did to pass the hours of the day and night. Morris even spoke of his feelings of failure to Aaron Hayman who he knew would repeat everything to his sons. Like Yankel, Aaron told Morris to accept the salesman job and make the best of it. "What choice have I got," Morris would reply. "But how's that going to stop me from seeing myself as I really am.'' ''Don't tell Erwin you feel this way,'' Aaron offered. ''Jack, maybe, but not Erwin. He worries that it will rub off on customers. Business first, personal feelings later—much, much later.''

Menachim too warned his father about telling others about his image as a failed man. It can't be good for any of us, Menachim advised him. What he wished he could say was that talk of failure scared him and made him feel he was destined to become a failure like his father.

Something else about his father's obsession with failure disturbed Menachim Kanter. Why was it that the job with the Hayman brothers brought forth such self-deprecation when everyone saw that Morris' health had begun to improve the instant he began working. To be sure, Morris was only a salesman earning less than the other salesmen, but his health had taken a surprising turn for the good. Even a little problem with his heart seemed to disappear.

In recalling that period, Menachim told a friend: ''Half of him got better, half of him got worse, but still it felt like he was infecting me with a strange disease. He was in good spirits. He complained about the low salary and how he was better than the other salesmen, none of whom knew half as much about the business as he did, but he raced through breakfast just like he did when he owned his own business. Failure, failure, failure. That's all he talked about. It was dangerous talk. I was too young to hear about all that, but I wonder whether he was all that depressed by it. It was like he was putting up this front. Owning your own business is the number one goal; working for someone else in a low capacity is failure. All right, everyone knows that, but he wanted to make sure everyone, and me especially, knew what real success and failure was all about. He didn't like the idea that he could be happy in a position he himself called a sign of failure. But he was sort of happy. He never talked to anyone about it. Maybe he thought no one would find out about it, so why tell them. God, what a difficult and complicated man!''

Morris Kanter always had been a private man who, while openly complaining of his troubles, told no one of the sadness in his life. Friends saw him as a hard working, tired, burdened man who had lived through a trying history. If he didn't want to discuss his life, why should they pry. What he needed, most agreed, was a woman. She didn't even have to be a wife or a mother for Menachim. But a man needs a woman to tell troubles to. Morris didn't need a replacement for his wife, he needed a friend. Yankel told him this a hundred times. ''You found all this out in your books?'' Morris chided his brother. ''Freud, no doubt, has some theory about it?''

''You don't go back,'' Yankel would say, ''but that doesn't mean you can't go forward. Nothing means forgetting the past, as if that were possible.''

Morris would look at him as if to say who the hell are we trying to kid! ''Our lives were spoiled. The greatest contribution is to make sure the next generation suffers as little as possible. Which means Menachim.'' Yankel never pursued the issue. He knew that eventually Morris would drag out the old argument: "It's easy for you, Yankel; you have nobody. All right when he's a man with his own family, but now he's a boy."

Yet Morris Kanter's happiness did indeed come from a woman, Fanny Boehm. When his wife died, Morris made a pledge he would never marry again. Every woman reminded him of Anna; every scene with a woman, every image he saw or imagined brought the memories back to him. There would never again be a woman, not even for Menachim's sake, as so many people gently advised him. "Of course he needs a mother," Morris would reply bitterly. "He needs *his* mother." But Fanny Boehm became a close friend. It all started innocently enough. Morris required a woman to look after the house when he still owned the stationery business. Yankel gave him the names of several women in the neighborhood who did occasional light work. Fanny Boehm was one of the women, although the most unreliable one, Yankel warned. Morris cared little about who cleaned, just as long as they didn't charge much. Fanny Boehm, as Yankel promised, was wholly unreliable. Morris would have fired her except that she convinced him that her irresponsibility was due to her frequent illnesses.

There was a sadness and loneliness about Fanny that Menachim at once detected, but she was a kind and decent woman. She was firm with the boy, and she maintained her dignity even when undertaking the most menial job. Quiet and keenly intelligent, she could reveal an unusually witty side. She spoke German and Dutch, as her own path to survival after incarceration in death camps had taken her to Holland where she worked as a washerwoman in the home of a doctor. The doctor not only employed her, but looked after her health. A victim of medical experimentation in one of the camps, Fanny was fortunate not to have died during the war and later in Amsterdam when a hysterectomy was performed on her and a large section of bowel was removed. In her early twenties, she too pledged never to marry now that she could no longer bear children. The war, moreover, had taken her ambition. Once a serious student of art with an eye to becoming a doctor, she gave up her plans and worked as a cleaning woman. Where she lived made little difference to her; the only thing that mattered was to serve well the people who had taken good care of her. Besides, as her family had been killed, it didn't make much difference what she became or where she became it.

When, exactly, the relationship between Morris Kanter and Fanny Boehm took on a more intimate tone was a matter known only by the two of them. Menachim suspected nothing until his last years of high school. His father occasionally came home late in the evenings or disappeared from the apartment on weekends, but Menachim always assumed he was playing checkers or catching up on work. But finally Morris told his son of his secret friendship with Fanny. The boy was pleased, his father embarrassed. Menachim wondered if his father planned to marry. Morris said he would never remarry. Fanny knew this and preferred it that way. They were just friends, two people with their private reasons for not wanting to be married. Yankel, however, was not to know of the involvement. Menachim promised to tell no one.

Sadly, for Menachim, what his father called "just an important friendship" did not result in Morris and Fanny spending more time with him. She
never joined them for dinner, although on the rare times that Menachim attended
schul on Friday evenings he occasionally spotted Fanny speaking with his father
on the corner near the temple. The only noticeable change was that Fanny ceased
working for the Kanters, which meant that a new cleaning woman was hired.
Jennifer Riley resented her work, although in Menachim's eyes she did very little
of it and complained about every speck of dust in the Kanter apartment.
Menachim would let her in on Saturday mornings, but when she began washing
the floors, he left and managed not to return until dinner. It had never been this
way with Fanny, whom he watched, fascinated by the motions of her work.

If the revelation of Morris' special friendship with Fanny made only insignificant changes in the Kanter's public life style, it aroused something very deep
in Menachim. Since his childhood, he was never wholly convinced that his
mother was dead. Granted, he recognized his wish to deny the fact, but he had
never seen concrete evidence of her death. The Nazis had taken her prisoner, and
when no one heard from her again, she was presumed dead. Thousands of
families had experienced the same thing. In times of war, disappearance implied
death. Still, Menachim wished he could visit her grave. They could make their
own pretend grave, his father told him once. They could treat it as a monument to
Menachim's mother. Menachim hated the idea and felt his father's suggestion to
be preposterous. Morris insisted that many people did just this. Not knowing the
location of a relative, they simply created a grave. It can be as holy a resting
place as a real grave, he entreated his son. The Rabbi would confirm his story.
Menachim was unmoved. Either they found his mother or her real grave, or they
did nothing.

Without the existence of a grave, it was only natural that Menachim grew
up believing in the possibility that his mother was alive. As a child, he dreamed
of spending his life hunting her down, just as intelligence operators spent their
lives tracking down war criminals. But there is a problem, he would think, lying
in bed. What if he discovered that his mother was alive and remarried, with
children? What if she had forgotten about him, or decided she would rather live
with her new family? What if she disappeared during the war because she never
really loved her husband and son? If Anna Kanter were alive, Menachim wondered, why had she not sought him out? It would have been easy for her to learn
precisely where her husband and son lived. Perhaps she had tried and was denied
the information. Yankel had told such stories in Menachim's presence. Perhaps
Kanter was not the true family name. Perhaps Morris and Yankel only took it to
rid themselves of the war memories. If Anna were alive, she would never be able
to find her husband.

Menachim's reasoning went even further. Any woman, he imagined, who
befriended his father or uncle could well be his mother. Afraid to upset him by
suddenly returning, she nonetheless wished to be close, if only to see how he was
growing up. Yankel had many women friends. Fanny Boehm, of course, could

have been her. In fact there was a resemblance between Fanny and Menachim. Morris noticed it, but Fanny remarked on it first. She said it was the reason she felt uneasy being around Menachim. When Menachim spoke to his father about the physical resemblance and its delicate connection to his childhood fantasies about his mother, he saw his father's eyes turn moist. "Maybe," Morris said, "that's a good reason for the three of us not living together." The words were spoken softly, but firmly. Menachim could tell he must not argue the point, even though he thought his father's logic to be senseless. If three people suffered from not having a family, why *not* live together. What was wrong with pretending they were a family. Even real families pretended. But Menachim never argued the point with his father. Morris was resolute: Business relationships were to be kept separate from his family relationships, and Fanny was to be kept separate from Menachim.

Bitter about his father's attitude on the matter, Menachim grew up believing he was beyond the point of caring all that much about whether or not his father would remarry. A boy needs a mother most when he is small, he told himself, and he had had his mother for the first two years. By the time he is fifteen or sixteen, a boy needs her barely at all. In fact, he might have had an advantage over some of his friends who spent no time with their fathers. Whatever he felt as a child, Menachim told no one of his sadness. Later in life, he could look back and reflect on just how unhappy he had been. To the outside world, however, he seemed no different than any of the children with whom he attended public school and Hebrew School. "That's the pain of middle age," he would say. "You know how you're feeling, and how you must have felt all your life. Worst of all, middle age means knowing how you're going to feel the rest of your life."

Morris Kanter's special friendship with Fanny Boehm evoked still another feeling in the young Menachim. If no one knew if his mother were alive or dead, and if he was only two when she disappeared and he was put into the care of various women, and if, as a child he never spent much time with his father, then how did he know for certain that Morris Kanter was truly his father? An unthinkable idea at one stage in his life, Fanny Boehm's presence turned the idea into an obsession. But whom could he speak to about this matter? Certainly not Yankel, for it would threaten his uncle just as it would his father. Possibly insane, the idea seemed just possible enough that Menachim cried when he thought of it too long.

Once, in school, Menachim's teacher asked the students to trace back their family history by interviewing their relatives. Students without living relatives were allowed to construct an imaginary family tree. At first, Menachim was terrified by the assignment. He told his friends the assignment was foolish and wasteful, but they disagreed with him. Only the young woman, Linda Orlovsky, with whom Menachim had become quite friendly, listened to him sympathetically. She knew little of Menachim's background, as he, like his father, was never one to speak about it. ''My father has a sationery business downtown,'' he told her. ''My mother died in the war.''

Linda Orlovsky could see that the family tree project had upset Menachim. She urged him either to tell the teacher he couldn't do it or invent a family tree. Nervous about having to raise the subject of his background with his teacher, Menachim chose to contrive a family history. He listed his grandparents as born in Germany. He showed his mother dead and the existence of three brothers and three sisters living somewhere in Europe. Various uncles and aunts, whom he indicated as being enormously wealthy, were residing in Canada and South America, except for his Uncle Yankel, whom he depicted as being married with three children. In addition to the invention of people, the chart made no internal sense whatsoever. In fact it was so bizzare that on the evening before it was due in class, Menachim tore it up, fell on his bed, and wept.

Moved, if not perplexed, by Menachim's unusual response to the assignment, Linda could not convince him to tell the teacher of his problems. Nor could she understand Menachim's inability even to imagine a family tree. Several years later, when both had completed high school and it appeared they would one day be married, Menachim admitted to his obsession with the idea that Morris was not his real father.

''Of course he's your father,'' Linda blurted out. ''Who else could he be?''

''He could be anybody in the world,'' Menachim answered flatly. ''Ask your mother about it.''

Linda did that very night, for she had marriage on her mind. And, although the Kanter's economic status would not be a deterrent to marriage, since her own family was hardly well off, there surely would be a problem if Menachim were mentally disturbed.

Rose Orlovsky's response to her daughter was forceful and direct. Linda remembered her mother as seeming more sturdy and thoughtful than ever before that one night.

''Nothing can be more tragic,'' Rose told her daughter, ''than for a child to be separated from his mother, especially when he is very small. But, when the separation occurs because the mother is dead . . . dead? When the mother's been killed in a concentration camp, then there can be no certainty about anything in that child's mind. Why should he believe anything anybody tells him about himself, or the person he's always believed was his father? Any child who's adopted wonders who his real parents are. If *you* want to find out, you go to city hall and look at the birth certificate with our signatures on it. I don't know, maybe they even fingerprint babies nowadays. But even if they don't, I *saw* you being born, we both saw you all the time. There's no way in the world that you aren't our real daughter. But how can Menachim know for sure about any of this. All the records were destroyed when he came to this country. Or maybe they weren't. Maybe there are records somewhere in Germany that could prove to him that his father is really his father. Many of these people don't even want to know about these things. They all think about it, but a lot of them wouldn't dare go back. And people like us and Mr. Kanter, do we have the money lying around to take a trip to Germany to go looking for records that maybe aren't even there?

"Any one of us, no matter how we grew, wherever we came from—and thank God your father and I didn't go through that experience—any of us can look at the world and say, 'I doubt everything. *Prove* to me that everything I see and hear and smell and touch really exists.' You could go crazy thinking like this, but you could go through life like this. Maybe we'd say a person thinking like this is a little nuts. But when a boy like Menachim thinks this way, it's natural. We *expect* him to think this way. After all, how does he know what he knows? The Nazis hurt him very deeply. They took his mother, they took away a lot of money, I understand, and they took away his ability to know anything for sure, maybe for the rest of his life. We just don't know."

By the time he reached his thirty-fifth birthday, Menachim Kanter was a profoundly unhappy man. There was nothing in his life he could look at and call a success. He felt blessed to have his wife, Linda. Many men, he recognized, would have been divorced by this point. He was not a good husband—a worse father. Something always kept him from being relaxed and natural with his son. Inevitably, he found himself judging David, no matter what the activity. A simple Saturday afternoon trip to the movies would start well enough, but eventually there would be tension. What the boy was learning always seemed more important to him than what David might think or feel. When David revealed a slowness or inability to catch on to something, Menachim became more than impatient. He would make it clear he was disappointed in his son. When he was small, David would cry from the frustration and feeling of discouragement. When he was older, he bit his lip and fought back the tears. Quite possiely he wasn't even aware of the anger he felt toward his father. Menachim, however, felt the anger. He knew that sometime in the future the stored up anger would have to come out. There was far too much tension in the house caused by Menachim's perpetual sense of hopelessness and his mother-in-law Rose's constant need to give advice.

"So, what do I do about it?" Menachim confronted me one day. "It can only go downhill, if my life hasn't already reached the bottom. What can be in the future. Someone's got a bunch of surprises for me when I turn forty, or how 'bout fifty? Now *there's* a great age to be when you've made absolutely no life for yourself. I don't know, like I say, but I'm willing to listen."

Menachim Kanter had few people with whom he could talk. Those who took a drink with him soon found his preoccupation with personal failure tedious. Men in similar financial positions, or even worse off, hardly needed to hear soulful laments from someone else; they could offer their own. I listened to Menachim as often as I could, and watched, as the months passed, his increasing depression. Sitting together on a park bench drinking cola, Menachim would say, almost without emotion:

"*You* tell *me* what I should stay alive for. I make my wife unhappy, I make my kid angry, I got nothing to say to Rose or my father, I've lost my strength, I'm being erased. You know how kids write with chalk on the sidewalk, and how maybe if they're lucky it will stay a couple of days? Then with the rain or people walking on it, it disappears? That's me. No one's doing it; it's just being done. I'm going to be forty years old in two years, and look at me. Look what I've built for myself. What have I done but make trouble for people, or sadness? You think my father's proud of what I am? And Rose, if I bought a house for us you think that would shut her up? The hell it would. She'd be back in a week talking better clothes, better jobs, better this. There's no end to it with her, you know.

"So, I just don't see that anybody can really give me a good lecture on why I should stay alive. Do it for your kid. That's what people always say. They said that for years about divorce too. You know how many unhappy people stayed together for the sake of their children when they *and* their children would have been better off if the parents had gotten a divorce? The best thing I could do for both of them would be knock myself off. She'd get remarried, and David, he'd be furious and bewildered for a while, but he'd get over it. He'd wonder about it, but he wouldn't have me around bitching and moaning. Life's not easy for him. I'll tell you something: My not having a mother has its effects on him too. He knows I hold a little resentment of the fact that he has a mother and I don't. He's got damn good reason to be angry. He says it himself; that he gets the short end of the stick because of what happened to me before he was even born.

"But it's my fault. Okay, the Nazis were bastards, the worst sons of bitches that ever walked the earth, but how long do you hold a grudge against people you've never seen? They killed my mother, we assume, so that's it. If she'd been hit by a bus, I could hold the same grudge against the bus driver. A kid has a mother, then something happens and the kid doesn't have his mother any more. It's forty years ago. Four decades! How long do I suffer over it. How long does it have to be one of the things that erases me. Take it another way. Maybe it's only partly my mother dying, maybe it's the way my father raised me. Okay, he didn't do all that great, so what, we survived. I never went hungry. I got a good enough education. I always had my own room, and just about anything I wanted. It wasn't the happiest house in the United States, but it wasn't an orphanage. I had religious training which I cared about; I'm a Jew, that's all good. So, where's the trouble? Why the hell do I have to be so upset about things that happened *decades* ago?

"You go up to a soldier. The guy's just sitting there on a road. He's got his pack and his gun, the whole schmear on the ground next to him. He's wearing his helmet. He hasn't shaved. Maybe he's smoking a cigarette, but he's sitting there all by himself. He doesn't even speak. Okay? Now, miles away from where he's sitting is his company. Bang, bang, boom, boom, they're fighting the war miles away from the guy. He knows where he is, where they are, and where he's *supposed* to be, but he's not there. 'Hello, Mendel, how come you're not fighting no more?' 'Don't want to.' 'What do you mean you don't *want* to? You *have* to!' 'I don't want to. I fought, tough, day and night, now I'm tired. I'm quitting.' 'But everybody else is tired too; they've been fighting just as hard as you and they're still at it,' 'Let 'em. I'm tired.' 'But you know what will happen to you if you stay here like this?' 'The war will be won or the war will be lost.' 'And you don't care?' 'A long time ago I did, but not any more.' 'But you can't stay here. It's against the law.' 'So they'll try me and shoot me.' 'Mendel, you're a coward.' *There's* the big punch line. You look down at this guy, and you frown, and you disapprove of him and you tell him, 'You're a Jewish coward bastard quitter.' And that's me. So shoot me or let me smoke my cigarette in peace!

"That's the first part of the story. Of course I'm the soldier sitting there. But I'm also the other guy who asks him all these questions and tells him he's a coward. I'm still that guy too. I ask myself those questions every day. The guy questioning the soldier? That's the little bit of life I have left. But pretty soon the story's going to change. The war's still going to be on, and the soldier's still going to sit there, waiting to die, but the guy who comes up to him asking all those questions, *he's* not going to be there any more. He's going to pass right by that soldier and he's going to tell himself, 'Let the poor old buzzard die.' If that's what he wants to do, it's nobody's business to try to change his mind. That's what it's come to. I don't want to talk any more about it. It's hard being *anything* when you're poor, but a lot of people do it. Some people are braver than me. I was brave for a while; four decades is a damn long time to put your strength behind something and come up empty handed. My father never got out of the past. I'm out of it. I'm going to get out of the present and future too. You just get tired.

"You want another example? Look at Israel. Nobody's more behind that country than I am. I'll back it right down the line. No one wants them there. Everyday somebody else says they're committed to drive them into the sea. If Israel does *this* it's no good, if they do *that* it's no good. But over there they're heroes. The young, the old, the kids, *everybody*! Everybody's for the cause. A billion-to-one odds against them, Israel wins. Next war, ten billion-to-one against them, they win again, only this time it's in fewer days. All the Jews for Israel, right? No more. People over there are quitting. They aren't cowards, but they're saying, 'I've done my share, I've killed or saw people get killed, now I'm tired.' They're leaving, too—war heroes, hard workers, good people. They're not becoming anti-Israel; they're just tired. The spirit is like the body. Sometimes it has to go to sleep and sometimes it just dies. Israel is losing a lot of people they don't want to lose: young people. They've had it. They look around and say, Who the hell needs this. I did my share, I put in my time. I'm still a Jew, I'm still pro-Israel, but I want out.' I've had it too. I'm still a Jew, I'm still a husband and a father. I'm still a son to my father, but I am very tired.

"You know Temple Bet Shalom on Greeley Place? It used to be crowded most of the time; now you can go there and you're lucky if there's ten people for a minion. Holidays people go, but mostly it's for old people. Last year the old rabbi, a tremendous bore, he died. So the temple committee brought in this young guy, Marshall Weissenbrod. Brilliant. The guy's wonderful. You know he's wonderful because the old men hate him, right?

"Anyway, I listened to this Weissenbrod, and he was good. He spoke Hebrew with a rotten accent but that was all right. I even thought, 'What a shmuck I was not to become a rabbi,' which was a lie because I never wanted to be a rabbi. You know what I used to think when I was David's age and I used to sit in temple? I used to think, poor kids grow up to become rabbis. Honest to God. Rich kids, I thought, learn Hebrew and study the torah so they'll be well rounded when they become doctors and lawyers and businessmen.

"Anyway, Rabbi Weissenbrod and I had a talk. I went up to him one day after service and I asked him, 'Can we talk?' He said 'Sure, why not?' Not about what, just sure, why not. Two hours I sat with the man, a guy my age. Poor kid? The guy comes from tremendous wealth. Both his parents are lawyers. He went to law school *and* studied to become a rabbi. A lousy synagogue like Bet Shalom, it can't have any money in the treasury, and here's this fabulous guy who's got time to talk to me. So I thought, maybe I'm wrong, maybe religion's the answer. You want to know what he told me? If you're out of energy, you look for it wherever you can. Inside yourself, outside yourself. You look to your wife, you look to your son, you look to your relatives, your friends, memories, ideals, anything. And if you can't find the strength and you've honestly made the best effort you can, then you can't find the strength, and no amount of sermonizing and praying will get it back for you. Okay? No mention of God. No mention of come to temple more often.

"I took his advice, the advice he gave by not giving any, and I started going to temple, once, twice, three times a week. I began reading again, doing a little praying. A lot of it came back from when I was a boy. I remembered my bar mitzvah, and the wedding ceremony, some of the blessings. I even celebrated with them in the temple for Simcha Torah. It was very nice. Because of Weissenbrod, I started going again, and for six months I felt good. I talked to God, God talked to me."

"What'd he say, Manny?" I asked softly.

Menachim was grinning. "He said I complain too much. I 'bourch' too much. Things like that. He told me to shape up or ship out. *My* God's a sailor—merchant marines, better." Menachim was on the verge of laughing. "Of course, no one spoke to me. I'm bad off but voices I don't hear, unless it's my mother-in-law giving lectures in the kitchen to my wife over coffee and these horrible danish she finds from the only traif bakery in the state. No, I told myself, I am what I am; I'll be what I'll be. If a man like Rabbi Weissenbrod can be so encouraging, respectful, then I don't need to look elsewhere. So I made pledges how in the New Year I'm going to be different, better. The drinker says he won't drink; the gambler says he won't gamble; the guy like me decides he'll have to live with what he has.

"So, for six months it got better. Nothing changes, but maybe you feel a little bit better about yourself. You sort of stay on top of yourself. For a while it works. Then, boom, like a kid going down a slide, you go right back where you were. Down the slide, and all you think about is how poor you are, and how lousy the Jews have it, and how you hate the rich. You think about your job, and your house, and the trouble your kid's getting into at school, and how the neighborhood's changing. Anything can set you off. Mail comes, a bill, you get depressed. No mail, not a hello from nobody, you get depressed. And I don't think about all the dead people in my life when I'm at the bottom of the slide? I don't try to imagine my mother? It's like the slide leads you down into all the garbage of your life.

"I can be realistic about all this. I'm an unhappy man. You know that, everybody knows that. And I don't like what I am. We're poor Jewish people. We have it bad because we're Jews, and because we are not financially or politically powerful. We have no resources. Weissenbrod knows it; we all know it. When you're in this situation, which is really not that different from what the Jews face in Israel, it makes you into a child. Rabbi Weissenbrod said the same thing. We're dependent, we're dirty, we're smelly, we're like children people don't want. Not only me, every person in the temple. Go there this minute, you'll see poor children. They may be in their seventies and eighties, but they're children.

"You want to make me a man, give me a job at twenty-five thousand dollars a year, you won't hear me complain again, you won't even see me. The job and the money and I can forget the past. I'll be the kid who climbs *up* the slide. You give me the job and there's no more coming down. Rich Jews know the same feeling. Plenty rich Jews still come by Bet Shalom, not only during the holidays either. They remember, or they read. But they aren't children. They come with their good clothes and the hundred dollar shoes, but they aren't children. People don't want to admit what they are. They're afraid. They think about what they *were*, and if that's terrible they pretend what they might be. But they don't face up to what they are this exact second."

Menachim's voice had grown loud but he showed no concern that people walking in the park might have seen or heard him. He was crying, like the little boy he was trying to convince me that he was, and that he wasn't at the same time. He kept wiping his eyes and his cheeks, but a moment later the tears were there again, but he never stopped talking. I said to him softly: "Come on, Manny, let's get out of here. We'll get something to eat maybe, some ice cream."

Menachim didn't budge. He sat on the bench, his body erect. He was still wiping away the tears. "You know what I feel? Like someone just told me my mother died. It's like all these years I've lived with the knowledge, but it wasn't ever a fact. Because it didn't happen in an exact minute, or an exact hour. It's like it's always been there. But right now I feel the moment of it actually came and went. Like, maybe she was alive all these years and just now I got the message. I never heard it before. It's just been there, but I can't remember anything; there's nothing to remember. I can't make it up the slide. I see the top, I see the kids waiting to come down, but I can't make it. It's too high, and I'm not big enough. I feel sorry for myself, sorry for what I've said about other people, for what I've done, what I should have done. I'm not going to make it. Can I go back even further? And if I *do* go back further, does that guarantee that I go up again? Does it balance itself off, ever? This can't be real. People aren't meant to have lives like this. Somebody must have written all of this somewhere.''

He looked at me, his eyes red from crying, his hands shaking slightly, but a small smile starting to form. "If nobody's written it yet,'' he said, "then you will. Right? I *will* be in a book somewhere so people can read it and say, 'What a poor slobbering fool.' So busy feeling sorry for himself, how can you have any respect for him. He's a putz. Climb up the slide, putznik, you'll see how the other half lives, how it doesn't have to be all bad. You got it bad, putz, but you make it bad too. Go ahead, climb the slide. Or are you ashamed to be seen as exactly what you are. Hey putz, can you look in a mirror and admit what you are? A poor Jewish putz. I've read enough about you to know I don't want to read any more. I'm closing the book on you, putz. I don't want you in my life. Go home, putz, cry over your mother and father, disappear, don't pester me.

"All right, story's over. We'll get ice cream. Big banana split, like a couple of kids. Come on, I'll treat *you* for a change, and for fifteen minutes we can pretend that all men are created equal.''

9

Just a Memory

The world of David Kanter, a fourteen-year-old boy with good looks, his father's slight build, his mother's soft green eyes not without their look of worry, as if he were some sort of fugitive, was a world of trouble. His great Uncle Yankel knew only parts of it; David's parents, a bit more. But no one wanted to speak of any of it. It was his parents I was thinking about as I approached the little restaurant where David and I had arranged to meet. Menachim had told me that David had agreed to see me if it just weren't at home.

"What's wrong with home?" I asked.

"How's me and his mother for starters," came Menachim's quiet response. "Listen, I'm lucky he's still willing to call himself a Kanter. You aren't going to get anywhere with him. Yankel thinks you're the answer."

"The answer to what?" I asked.

"Oh, you know," Menachim's voice sounded wistful.

I felt embarrassed. "I'm supposed to be so great with a kid I don't even know?"

"Listen," Menachim saved me. "*I* didn't say you were great. It's your pal, Yankel."

"Tell me, Manny," I asked my friend, "what the hell is going on with David that I don't know about, or am supposed to know about or not know about?"

"What's not going on?" he answered flatly.

"You want to know something, Mr. Kanter," I began, letting him hear my own frustration, "I'm beginning to think that that business of Jews answering a

question with a question is true. Goodbye. I'll talk to you in a few days.'' I
started to hang up the phone.

"Where you meeting David?'' Suddenly Menachim's voice was alive again.

"Guido's.''

"Such a shabby place.''

"Is it?'' "You know, Manny, you really are becoming a pest. I'll send you
a bill. Okay? You happy?''

"Do it. Send a bill.''

Menachim's way with his friends never changed. He could accept nothing
for free. Everything, he insisted, had a price, and if he didn't pay he was being
treated as a poor man, and this fact tore at his heart. To get free what others paid
for was patronizing, pure and simple. If I told him once I told him a thousand
times, "Menachim, I shall not see David as a patient. I only want to meet him,
befriend him. If we think he should see somebody and he agrees, I'll get somebody for him.''

"But not too expensive,'' Menachim would interject, "and you must let
me pay you.''

David Kanter stood outside Guido's on a day when more rain fell on
Boston than anyone could remember. People were rushing anywhere to get
inside, under cover. It wasn't cold for April—just wet, miserably wet. But David
waited outside, barely protected by a small metal awning, the rain dripping onto
his gray hat and leather jacket.

"David?''

"You my dad's friend?''

"Tom.'' I pushed him gently inside. "You eat?''

"No.''

"You want to?''

"Yeah. I don't care. S'up to you.''

I threw my coat over a chair as we sat down. "You get a load of this day?''

"It's just rain,'' he answered softly. "April showers bring May flowers.''

"Not with this much water,'' I said good naturedly.

"I don't know much about it. I don't care for flowers. They got good pizza
here. You like pizza?''

"Yeah, I could go for a pizza,'' I said, my tone hopelessly artificial, as
though I honestly believed there were no problems in the world any more.

"I'll have a hamburger.''

There was some resemblance between the boy and his parents. But what
was so important, I wondered, about his resembling his parents? Why was the
relationship between Yankel, Morris, Menachim, and David so significant? So
they were uncles and nephews and sons and fathers. For this discovery, as
Yankel would say, you don't win medals. But surely Yankel would have had
some words about the beauty of families merely succeeding and surviving. His

own wife and children had perished in a Polish death camp, as had Morris' wife, Menachim's mother.

I found myself studying David's face, his long straight hair, the ringlets made by the dampness, his thin nose, the high cheekbones, the full lips and sorrowful eyes, the eyelids that rose slightly with their delicate hint of a fold. I felt his anger, the confusion, the fact that neither one of us had yet defined what this conversation was to be about. Perhaps I had decided already that he wouldn't let me be his friend. The sentiment was safer than admitting to myself that perhaps I didn't want to be close to him.

There's a time bomb in you, David, I said to myself. I hear the ticking. Whether it's going to go off, *that* nobody can say, not even you, David, who are trying so hard to convince people the world is terriffic and you're in command of everything. I know you now five minutes, and I sense it. I'll be damned if I know what it is, but I'll also be damned if I'll treat you as though it weren't there. You want to stand outside and let the rain fall on you, that's your business. Me, I'm staying where it's nice and warm.

"So what do you want to talk to me about?" David was asking.

"Just wanted to get to know you," I said.

"What for?"

Because you're driving your parents sick, I wanted to say, and because there's a man named Yankel Kanter, you've heard of him perhaps, who insists he won't go to his grave until he finds out what is making you so tough and uncontrollable, and unhappy.

"My father wants me to talk to you. I know that."

"Yes, he does." Your father's a good guy, I thought. A good friend. He's gone through a lot, and come from people who've gone through a lot.

"My mother talk to you too about how I'm difficult to get along with?" David's derision was as subtle as the smell of pizza in Guido's. "Poor Mom, she can't control her only son. She tell you that?"

"Not in so many words." Did your Mom talk to me? No David, your Mom *wept* to me. All right? You want to know the truth? Yankel's up here, your Grandfather's over here, your Dad's over here, your Mother's over here, your Grandmother Rose is over here, and in the grave, flesh rotten into the emptiness of coffins, is one Grandmother and one Grandfather. That's just in case you forgot the cast of characters. And that's what it is to you, too, new friend. Because in the extraordinary wisdom of all your combined fabulous fourteen years, you see all this Jewish history, this little Jewish family life as a great big drama, a routine, acts repeated every night, dinner-time performances at six-thirty when the old man gets home from the work he performs which brings in too damn little money for you.

David was shaking his head. "Poor Mother."

"I don't think she feels like a poor mother," I replied matter of factly. So who do you like, David, Lady Macbeth, Gertrude, maybe Ophelia? You want me to tell you how your mother wept when she spoke to your father and me one Saturday afternoon when nobody knew where you were and they feared you had gotten into trouble? All she wants, David, is for her husband and her only child to be happy; to accept what they are and do the best they can; then she'll be happy. Cloth coats instead of mink, no cars instead of a Cadillac, a two-bedroom apartment instead of a suburban home with a lawn, a body without a womb instead of a body intact? Does she tell you about any of these choices?

"My parents are really something, aren't they." David's mouth was filled with hamburger. "And Yankel, who acts like a famous rabbi and spends his time thinking about the war and how horrible it was because he's so afraid if he doesn't think about what happened maybe he'll forget about it and believe it was all just in his imagination."

Yankel Kanter created Hitler. Did they not tell you this, David? Oh yes. Hitler went to your great uncle and said, "Nu, Yankel, I've had an idea for a political program I'm calling National Socialism. A good term, don't you think?" "Beautiful," Yankel said respectfully. "Anyway, to launch it in just the right way for the whole world to see, I've come up with what I think is a tremendous idea; I'm calling it a holocaust." "I love it," Yankel said. "Don't tell me what it means. For a minute, I just want to savor the word. What do you think it'll cost?" "Close to six and a half million," Hitler said. "A little steep," Yankel replied. "But what the hell, nothing comes cheap. And when you want the whole world to sit up and take notice, the cost has to be high."

"I guess my family worries about me," David was saying. "I guess I give them reason to worry once in a while. Although not as much as they make me think. I do a little, they worry a lot. They worry about me getting into trouble when I sleep, for Chrissake. They never get off my back."

With each sentence, practically, his tone would change. First anger, then penitence, then anger all over again. There was nothing I could have done or said, I felt, that would have allowed us to become friends. It wasn't happening, and as I began to see it, *I* was to blame. I had gone to meet David Kanter prepared not only to dislike him, but to prove to him that he was a disloyal son, grandson and grand nephew, a disloyal Jew! I had unconsciously built an entire case, as a prosecuting attorney might, to demonstrate before a public court that this boy was a disgrace to himself, his family, me! There is always a danger of one's prejudgments arising in the process of conversations—any conversations. But one watches for these and tries to guard against them. I was watching out as usual, but finding myself indulging in the most primitive feelings I could ever remember having in the course of conducting my research. I wanted to be intensely Jewish in those minutes with David; knowledgeable, wise, talmudic, Jewish. And he, for good and understandable reasons, hadn't thought of the word Jewish for the entire time we spoke. I found myself staring at David's lovely face, imagining how he might look at my age. His hairline would never recede, the wrinkles in the forehead and around the eyes would make him appear more sensuous and kind, more intense, and a heavy beard would tell something else about him.

"You have a talis, David?"

"Sure."

"Wear it for your bar mitzvah?"

"You have to."

"That's right, you have to."

"You Jewish?"

"Yes."

"What's your last name again?"

"Cottle."

"You change it?"

"No. Doesn't sound too Jewish, eh?"

"I don't know."

"My being Jewish make any difference?"

"About what?"

"Anything. I don't know. Talking."

"Why should it?"

"Just wondering."

"Make any difference to you?" He never even looked up when he asked the question. Head down, fingers rummaging about in the hamburger crumbs and film of grease on his plate.

"Probably, in some way," I answered.

He said nothing.

"You want to know how it makes a difference?" I asked.

"You want to tell me?"

"Well, I won't dwell on it, but I got the impression from speaking with your family that you preferred not to be friends with other Jewish kids."

"So?"

"So, maybe that says something about your feelings about being Jewish."

"Maybe it does." He looked about the room without letting his eyes fall on me. Suddenly his face turned toward me and I found his eyes, mysteriously darker than they seemed before. His hair was drying, growing fluffy, and I swear that he looked older.

"Look, Mr. Cottle, meeting here wasn't my idea. And the way you've been talking it sounds like it probably wasn't your idea either. You're the big friend of Yankel's and my father's. So they probably told you; look, go talk with sick old David 'cause he's always in trouble. David's not a good boy. David's not a good Jew. He was bar mitzvahed and he went to Hebrew school, which he hated, but he isn't a good Jew. He doesn't do so great in school like Jewish boys are supposed to do, right? And he doesn't have a lot of Jewish friends like he's supposed to do, right? So talk to him, straighten him out; you're some kind of a shrink, aren't you? I'll bet that's what they said too. I don't want to disappoint you, but they say it to everybody who'll listen to them, especially Yankel. He's always worried about me. He always has books for me to read about young people this, young people that. The history of the Jews, the history of World War Two, Israel. I don't care about any of that stuff. They wanted me to be bar mitzvahed, so I'm bar mitzvahed. They don't honestly think anybody in the world any more actually believes that once you go through that nonsense you're really a man? Even with all their problems they must see that kids see right through these ceremonies. You do it for *them*, not yourself. I never once gave a flying shit about any of it. I thought it was the biggest waste of time in my life. If I had to go into the army when there wasn't even a war, I'd find *that* more interesting than getting bar mitzvahed.

"But they said, 'Do it for Yankel, do it for Grandma Rose and Papa Morris. Do it for the memory of this one, or that one.' *Why*? Why should I do things all the time just to please them? If that's the trouble they think I'm causing then I don't happen to think it's getting into trouble. All these people think the same thing: If you're Jewish, you're special, you're better than everybody else. You're even better, they think, if you're a Jewish criminal. You know how many Jews are involved in crime? Hundreds. Thousands of them probably. But no, Yankel or Grandma Rose, they teach you, Jews don't break the law. Jews don't fail. Who they trying to kid? *They're* the ones who failed; they made their own children into failures . . .

"Yankel has no children," I interrupted unthinkingly. My tone was quiet, but rude.

"Okay, not Yankel," he allowed, "but all the others. They never make it big so they want to make sure my generation won't be like them. So they push and push and when the kids don't end up like they want them to, they weep and cry and send for guys like you.

"You want to know the trouble I get into? We got black kids going to our school. I got nothing against them being there when they live near here. But when they don't, then I think they should stay away. My father doesn't like the idea that I don't want new ones coming into the school. It's not good when Jews talk this way. That's what my family always says. But why not? I'm not any different from anybody else. They're really hypocritical about it. Like, what happened to Yankel and my grandfather, that has nothing to do with me. That's years ago. Why should that have anything to do with what I feel about black kids coming into my school? You want to know what it is? It's that Jews being special business of theirs, and I'm more honest than they are about it. Almost every white kid I know doesn't like the idea of black kids coming into the school. They live with it, but if they had a choice, they wouldn't vote that way. But not the Jewish families. They're for integration. Ask my parents. So how come, if they're white, they don't agree with other white families in the school? Simple. Because rich families in the suburbs are *for* integration and the Jewish people, like in this neighborhood, want to pretend they're more like the suburban families than they're like the families who live around here. So they talk about how special and different Jews are. That's the hypocritical part because they don't like to think of themselves as not well off. All my father ever talks about is how he's poor, how he wishes he was living in the suburbs. He can't stand the idea that he isn't special.

"Jews aren't special. The *rich* are special. Nobody's special around here. But the Irish families and the Polish families and the others, they don't go pretending they're rich. My *cause* isn't the Germans or concentration camps or whatever they talk about. And I don't know whether I'm going to be rich or famous or poor and maybe even dead two hours from now. Everybody cares what happens to them, except people like Yankel whose whole life ended a long time ago. Maybe it would have been better if he died with his wife. He hasn't done anything particularly great since he came to this country. But he's like the rest of them. They don't like being short of money, and the whole world passing them by, which is what it's doing because they live in the past.

"It's like they think they're better than all these other people. First, they tell us we shouldn't mix with Christian families. Then they say we shouldn't mix with rich families. I don't know who they want me to be friends with. My mother always says, 'How come you don't bring kids home with you?' Well, first off, kids my age don't bring other kids home with them that much. And next, my mother's always so fussy about the kind of person I bring home, I stopped doing it because you never know with her whether these kids are going to pass her test. She spends too much time judging people, seeing whether they're right for us. I'm not going to do that. If I like somebody, I'll be friends with them. Doesn't make any difference to me whether they're Jewish or not. In fact, sometimes I think the non-Jewish kids are better 'cause they aren't so hung up on religion. Now, what else am I supposed to talk about?"

David had left me speechless. To see him sitting there, slouched in his chair, one would never suspect he could have delivered such a statement. He was not expecting me to respond. If I desired to come back with a lecture of my own, he was braced for that, but my words would bounce off him. It's a strange expression, "getting through" to someone. The phrase implies the presence of some sort of shield, a tangle of telephone wires. The scene was as proverbial as one could conceive; we were four feet from one another but we might as well have been separated by a million miles. "That's a helluva speech," I heard myself say.

"You like it," he said, leaning forward, "here's another one. This one's dedicated to my father. You and he are friends, so none of this is going to be new to you. But if you want to know what's on my mind about him, I'll say it."

David could tell from my expression that I was eager to hear what he had to say. What he didn't know was the uneasiness I was experiencing. In all the years of interviewing, sitting opposite another person, hearing them speak about their lives, there have been innumerable occasions when I disagree profoundly with some utterance, some opinion. So we will argue, fight it out with words, ideally ending up as friends, a bit closer perhaps than before, although a bit farther apart too in some instances. But with David, a new feeling had been evoked in me: No matter how I turned his words over in my head, they kept making *me* feel ashamed.

"You want to hear what's wrong with my father? He thinks there's only one way to be if you're Jewish, and that's rich. He'd never admit it, but he feels a Jew who isn't successful or a somebody shouldn't be alive probably. He doesn't expect anything of his father and Yankel, but he sure expects everything of himself. He's killing himself too. *He* thinks he's normal about everything he does. But the only thing he ever thinks about is how there's no reason for him to be doing as badly as he is. He hates himself. I go to school with lots of guys whose fathers left their families, you know. And those guys weren't half as bad off as my father. In fact, most of them were a whole lot happier than he is. There's no excuse for it, there's no excuse for it, that's all I ever hear him say.

"My father can't stand living where we live. He hates the neighborhood, our house, the other people who live in the building. They make too much noise, or they don't do anything with their lives. Every three months he comes up with a new plan for moving. First, we're going here, then we're going there. Then the two of them start clipping ads for houses out of the newspapers. They're like a couple of children cutting out paper dolls. They can't expect anyone to believe they're really going to buy anything when they barely have enough money to live where we live now. They just do it to sort of pretend they could change their life whenever they want to. They even go looking at the high schools. 'You want to come along, David? See what it looks like out there?' Why the hell should I go? I'm never going to go to one of those schools, so what's the point in looking at them! Or they'll say, 'There's a good temple and a nice Jewish community.' That's always very important. One time I told him, 'How come you do this when you know you're never going to buy a house?' He said he was just about to put a down payment on a house when he found out from somebody there was a lot of strong anti-Jewish feelings in that community. I didn't believe him for a second. If he had the money but the house he wanted was a thousand miles from another Jewish family he'd buy the house.

"I don't hate him for what he's trying to do. I feel sorry for him. I hate them when they lie. And I can't stand him lying to himself. He's killing himself pretending he's going to make it someday when everybody knows he'll never be better off than he is now. Guys like my dad were never meant to be rich. He thinks they are because most Jews are successful at no matter what they try. But he's no different from other men around here. If he ever stopped to talk to them he'd find out he's just like them. I wouldn't say he's stuck up. What he is is a working class guy who never had—never will have—enough money, who's afraid to be seen by a non-Jew who's going to ask him, 'If you're Jewish, how come you aren't rich?'

"Lookit, Mr. Cottle, this can't be the best thing you got to do with your time is come around a place like this and talk to a kid like me. I mean, I'm not sure what you do, but whatever it is you must have better things to do with your time. Especially when it rains." David glanced toward the windows. The rain had subsided.

"I'm perfectly content being here with you, David."

"Suit yourself. All I wanted to say was that if you want to know what's going on in my family, the person to talk to is my father. Maybe my mother a little, too. I don't have anything. I'll be all right, even though Yankel and my father are convinced I'm going to end up in reform school. I don't know what I do that gives them that impression. Sometimes you'd think they have me sized up to be the Jewish Al Capone or something."

David was shaking his head when suddenly he began staring at the people huddled in the doorway. They were looking out, hoping for the rain to stop. His brows furled, a muscle in his cheek twitched. He reached a hand up to silence it, then quickly looked to see whether I had noticed him.

"You know those people, David?"

"They reminded me of when I was small, like five or six. We had a sucot, you know what that is?"

"Yes."

"My father and Yankel built it behind our apartment building, near the back stairs where they keep the garbage cans. They did a great job too, because knowing on some of the days you celebrate sucot it has to rain, they fixed it so people could go into it without walking outside. Everybody went into it, too, the entire building. Old people were in there, and babies. It was terrific. Anyway, one of the nights it rained. Everybody was waiting for the thing to come down, it was only made of canvas and rope. We were sure the wind would blow it away, which was really too bad since my mother and Mrs. Perlman had made all this food. We had furniture in there, too. Everyone was disappointed because my father and Yankel had worked so hard, and the women had spent so much time making food, but nobody wanted to leave. We were like those people at the door, looking up, almost praying the weather would get better, or the sucot would blow away.

"Then my father stood up and told everybody not to worry. He said no wind would blow it over and the places where it leaked wouldn't cause any problems. Nobody seemed to worry any more after that. My father told them they'd be all right, and they believed him. We all sat around and ate. Everybody had a wonderful time, even though it got so dark nobody could see that well. The candles we had kept going out. I had to keep going up to our apartment to get more. I actually had a great time running after candles. My father kept telling me to bring all the boxes down with me so I wouldn't have to make the trips but I didn't want to. I loved running up in the dark, groping around, you know, going to the kitchen, getting the candles, feeling my way down the stairs into the basement which always was such a scary place for me, except that night, or that week really, when they made the sucot. Everybody applauded when I came back, and my father lit a candle. Then it would be light, while this one little candle, which *I* had carried down, would flicker. Then it would go out and everybody would groan and pretend to be sad. So my father would light it again and we'd be happy again as this tiny little orange light came into the sucot. I remember they had lovely colors painted on the canvas. It was really beautiful. Everybody stayed there and forgot about the weather, and my father was the most important person there because he was the one who made the sucot. It's amazing how you see people standing in the doorway and all those memories come back, although you'd think since that was such a nice time I'd remember it more often. So you think I'm crazy?''

"That's a very touching story," I said quietly. "I don't have recollections of being in a sucot as a child."

"I don't think it's all that much." David's toughness had returned. "Maybe you just like it 'cause it makes me sound like Yankel and my father want me to be. If I went to schul every day they'd think I was the greatest guy in the world, even if I ended up flat broke. It was just a memory. We haven't had a sucot in years, thank God!"

I lifted my head and nodded. Well David, that's the way it is with some memories and dreams. They return to us almost by accident, it seems, night travellers knocking on doors with the light so dim they can barely see, believing they have found their own homes, when, by accident, they have reached a prior home, the home of their childhood perhaps.

"Are we done?" I barely heard him ask.

"If you like."

The afternoon was over. He refused my invitation to drive him home. We shook hands and went out into the rain in opposite directions. In minutes I was caught in evening traffic, the piercing white lights of the cars and the outlines of tired, frustrated drivers trapped in their machines. David was walking. He would be home before I even made it to the next blurry red light. You're lucky, my friend, I whispered. You have all those people who love you. So they worry about you, so what. You want love, you need love, you get it! You cannot dictate the form in which it comes. Lots of people want something, but won't settle for just any form of it. These people have to be told, you'll get what you'll get when it's available. I'm an expert on this type of person, David, because I am one of them.

And David, about that time bomb metaphor. I'm sorry for it. It was a premature assessment, as patronizing as it was presumptuous. Forgive me for it. Forgive me, too, for still believing that a bomb is there. Forgive me for siding with Yankel and your father. But I'm worried about you.

___10___

The Abandoners

Memory works in a miraculous way. If one experiences some momentous event, for example, or receives important news, or maybe engages in a poignant or powerful meeting with someone, one's memory is able to bring back much of the extraneous data: the weather of that day, or maybe the clothes one was wearing, or what one was doing just before or following the event. Like activated electromagnets, memory cells collect whatever they can and meld these once displaced bits into a cluttered but still succinct recollection. It was only natural, then, that I should be able to recall easily the event sof my meeting with Mr. Malcolm Holden.

For about two and a half years, I had worked with Johnnie Holden. When he was sixteen, he had been picked up by the police for stealing—just one guy in a bunch of young people looking for something exciting to do one night—and from that point on we had become friends. We talked a lot, this husky young man and I—about the technical school he attended, about books and girls, and the future, which at the time seemed precarious and uninviting. Soon he was visiting the University, meeting some students, being tutored in three subjects, and gradually being ''prepped'' by all of us for college and whatever college might bring.

There was a lot of talk during those nights about the ethics of working with lower-class youth, imposing one's values and sense of fortune and triumph on them, and listening to their needs. But during the day, we all resumed our collective efforts to get this one young man, and others as well, ready for examinations and college application forms. A number of people spoke with his parents who, word had it, were delighted by the idea that a group of university people who previously had paid no attention to "the community" was about to transform *their* son over night into a middle-class success story. Their objections and reservations resembled our own nightly debates. Perhaps John should stay with his own crowd, move where it moved, following its own preordained cultural tempo. University students were too smug, perhaps, or maybe they corrupted young people like Johnnie Holden.

But did our efforts in the late 1960s in fact mean that young, punk college students were trying to tell forty-year-old parents that they didn't know how to raise their children? What did we know, after all, about labor pains, trips to hospitals with sick children, digging for money to pay bills or staying up all night with crying, nagging sons and daughters? Oh, God no, the parents had been assured by someone, we were told, that these are great kids who love Johnnie. They're learning a great deal from him just as they're trying to help him with his school work. "I know you saw his report card," I imagined someone saying to his mother. "He's really doing a whole lot better and staying out of trouble too, and there's a mob of fabulous kids over here who help each other in ways that the schools either don't allow for or maybe just can't accept. Look, Mrs. Holden," someone surely would have said to her, "we don't want to take your kid away from you in that way. That's not our purpose at all. In fact, it's just the antithesis, you know, the opposite of what we want." And she would say, I imagined, "Yes, yes, I know, but you can understand how it is, how I feel . . . We don't go there, and we see John so little these days . . . and Malcolm always gets a bit huffy . . . You have to understand how he feels about all of this help you're giving. He *is* his father . . ."

And then it would start, for I would say to myself behind Malcolm Holden's ugly undershirted back, which he surely had and which he surely wore when he watched his mindless television programs and drank his beer: "Lookit, Mr. Holden, if you don't like what we're doing to your kid, then why the hell don't you come over here once? Just once, man, and see with your own eyes whether or not you *approve* of our little program. If you're so goddamned huffy about the fact that maybe we just happen to be taking a helluva lot more interest in your kid these days then you seem to be, then get over here some night instead of watching that goddamn crap on TV. If you care so much, Mr. Holden, why don't you spend a little more time with your own son? You wanna know the truth, Mr. Holden? I don't give a rat's ass if you happen to be older than I am. I'm taking time out of *my* life, time out of *my* work to be with *your* kid. And I don't care whether you call it therapy, tutoring, counseling, middle classing, or pumping up his motivation. So I'm rich and guilty and I wanna help some poor kid make it a little. You don't like it, Mr. Holden? Sue me. I'll find myself another kid, one who'll be glad to have me to latch onto once in a while when just being a boy or being sixteen is too hard. Fact is, Mr. Holden, I'll get myself a kid with a father who doesn't drink, and who doesn't clobber his wife, like maybe three, four times a week, huh? . . . huh? . . . and who doesn't have that Nellie woman on Houghton Street near the Spa where he goes every other Friday to drink . . . huh? . . . What do you say, Mr. Holden? You feeling a little guilty yourself? What's that face of yours look like now, Mr. Holden? A little red just once, just once from embarrassment, maybe, and not from *BOOZING?* You know how many times I've talked to your kid about your drinking? How it scares the shit out of him? You know about that? You want to know what we talk about when we walk into the Square on Thursdays to buy ice cream or along the bank of the Charles, not that far, incidentally, from where you work? You wanna know, dad? I'll tell you. I think you oughta know! I think you oughta know what your depressed, frightened son says about his homelife which, more than any-thing else, means his life with you. Not with teachers or police. With you! So let's start with you and your notions about child rearing and punishment. Then let's move on to your ideas about being a father, like throwing your kid out of the house for days on end and making him find someplace to live. You think all you have to do is ball some woman, drop your load and that makes you a father? That's what it means to you, Mr. Holden? Wham bam, thank you ma'am? And do you think you can beat her just 'cause she's your wife? Draw blood from her nose and ears and mouth, and then walk over to Nicky's and pour booze down your throat and get so bombed you can barely find Nellie or Mollie or whatever her name is, and have your six-year-old son and your three-year-old boy wipe up the blood and get your wife who must be, what, one hundred and fifty pounds, into bed? Two kids, who together can barely move an easy chair, lifting this half-conscious woman into her bed, and cleaning her up and cleaning up the house, and comforting her. And then, and this part makes me sick inside, Mr. Holden, setting the table for dinner just the way the old lady—isn't that what you call her?—had set it before you came along with that little boy anger of yours and just about destroyed the whole goddamn house. And all the while you're drinking away so innocently or sleeping with a woman. Now, Mr. Holden, do you really think that these two boys are gonna have any confidence, any pride, any sense of decency and security? What's more, you think that guilty or successful or what-ever I am, that I'm gonna sit in my office ten blocks from your home and let all this happen to your son without batting an eye? Because if you do, if you think I'm not furious with you and that I wouldn't like to adopt that Boston-sounding kid of yours, even with his ignorance and intolerance, his hatred of people that I care very much about, if you think I wouldn't like to send him underground somewhere where you wouldn't know where to get your hands on him, then you're crazy, wrong, out of your mind. Then, Mr. Holden, you're even more stupid than I once thought, and I got news for you, Mac, I never thought too much of you in the beginning! But someday I'm going to meet you face to face and I'm going to tell you *my* side of the story. I'm going to tell you about what your son does in his free time, and where he goes when you can't stand his face at home, and how if we didn't intervene, upgrade him or whatever you'd like to call it, he'd end up not only with your last name, but with an existence exactly like yours. Everything just like you! So, what I've decided, Mr. Invisible Malcolm Holden, whose life is so terribly busy and whose obligations are so much more important than my own measly little pedestrian chores, is that psychiatric and social science ethics and procedures can all go to hell! Suddenly I don't care about protocol and proper demeanor with *the parents*. What've you been doing all these weeks? Why don't you return just one of the phone calls we've made to your home? How come you can't figure out that it's because of decency and protection of your son that we call you at home and not at work? D'you ever stop to think of that? I swear to you, when we meet I'm going to forget all those cumbersome professional ethics and let you know where I stand on real issues. Not on the working class and flag burning and demonstrations and all the rest. Hell no. You and I are going to talk about your son, who I swear to God we're going to try to make so middle class, so upper middle class, so upper class WASPish you aren't going to recognize him even *if* he ever comes home on Christmas vacations, which I also might try to discourage. He'll never get to Vietnam if we have anything to say about it; he'll never do what you do; and if he wants to sit in his college room every night and smoke pot and make plans for a Gay Liberation Movement that would make you, no doubt, shit in your pants, then that's what he's going to do and I'm going to love it. I'll tell you something. The way I feel about you, I hope that's exactly what your kid does, because he's developed, shall we say, a little hatred toward you over these last fifteen years, and maybe just a little has rubbed off on me. Do I make myself clear, or would you like me to run it again from the top?''

Johnnie Holden *did* make it to college. In fact, when decisions were announced, he was choosing among four schools, two of which had offered him magnificent scholarships. Everyone knows, surely, how we felt. John himself was ecstatic. There was a lovely party for him, and then, all at once, it was over. The elation and the anger, the hours of tedium and effort and motion and no motion were gone. The boy, too, was gone, and surprisingly we did not keep in touch. Some requests from him came to us, a bit of news, too, though usually through other people, but in the main, it was over, and we were left alone, believing that maybe something was owed us; from the boy's parents, from the government, a medal from the President, something.

Actually, it is from the boy himself that one would like to hear a little something. Is this, finally, what parents suffer with? Is this the feeling produced by weeks of silence when the children go off to school? Is this what they mean when they say maybe you could write now and then, or call us, you can always call us collect, you know; or when they tell you it's so silent here, we're rattling around in this big house all by ourselves? Well, one gets older, and one always has his work, his daily activities that keep him in-the-world, attached, responsible, a contributing, productive citizen.

Then, suddenly, a call came from a friend. Mrs. Holden had called him. Now it was Peter Holden, John's younger brother.

At fourteen, Peter David Holden was a tall, lovely young man with smooth, light-brown hair; a person with a most ingenuous love for good books, and an uncanny capacity for differentiating between good poems and great poems, good novels and great novels. Within a week he had come to me with a poem written by Gerard Manley Hopkins. He read it aloud as we drank tea in a Cambridge pastry shop, and I could see that he had practically memorized the entire work. What a beautiful boy, and flunking every course in school, including English and social studies where truly he knew everything. He was cutting classes every day, disappearing at examination time and, all told, showing up in that ugly fortress of a high school no more than three hours a week. No one knew where he went or how he lived. No one knew the whereabouts of "the streets" he referred to so often.

It is unbelievable what happens to some people, I would think as we sat together talking about poetry: "and told of her beauty, and praised her simply and frankly as though she were a fable of the bards; and he asked her humbly to give him her love, for he was only subtle in his dreams." There is such a peculiar agreement made in these kinds of friendships. Here am I, and there's the young man, and I know that something profound is troubling him, and he knows that I know, but still a little time has to be spent before he can share the sadness, or even harder, before he can reveal the anger towards loved, if not revered people. A bit of time must be allowed to pass, for if we rush into it we fail to protect those whom we love, despite ourselves, and thereby make them seem much worse than they really are; worse, that is, than we want them to be.

So while there is an urgency on both our parts, we let time play itself out. We talk a bit and walk together, and, like soldiers in the dark, silently exchange the messages of our intensity, commitment, and emotionality. Through him I once again begin to feel that primordial fury that comes when one hears about the pain of youth that only fathers, we believe, in their petulant, drunken and bitter moments can cause; the anger that comes from seeing the young falter, and from hearing of their periodic disappearances which alert the world to their own anger, to their wishes for death, someone's death somewhere, and their wishes for attention and loving communion. The boy himself had advised me that his own depressions were coming more often and lasting longer.

There were always young men, neighborhood pirates, who would have called Peter Holden a "beautiful cat" had he possessed the same qualities but used them perhaps in slightly different ways. Despite the genuine openness of youth that we hear and write about, the young often exhibit less endearing qualities. In Peter's neighborhood, a bunch of toughs felt that Peter was a "weirdo," a queer surely, because he got caught one day when a good-natured punch knocked him to the ground between two parked cars on Broadway. Among the things that fell out of his notebook was a piece of yellow lined paper with a passage from a narrative poem by Pushkin which Peter had copied. They razzed him about the name Pushkin and danced around him, so he described, this group of friends who mattered so desperately to him that they could convince him to follow them into their maniacal adventures and even work to depress his intelligence and sensibilities. They danced about him, and he, not for a moment able to envision a world without their influence, guidance and reckless support, rolled about with affected laughter and specially prepared adolescent masculine embarrassment, even when in the middle of the sidewalk they read with the most outlandish voices they could possibly muster:

> My words may move some unborn lover;
> My stanza, saved by jealous fate,
> It may be Lethe will not cover;
> Ah yes, at some far distant date,
> When I am gone, and cannot know it,
> The cordial words: "There was a poet!"

"Listen, sweetie," they limp-wristed him, and flung their denimed hips, "you wanna go out on a . . . on 'some far distant date' with me? Huh, sweetie?"

"Come on, Petey boy, you little poet, you sweet, lovely little dreamer." And then, with a crescendo of their voices, "YOU FUCKING QUEER!" Peter listened for their every word, their every evaluation, and watched for each gesture that bespoke the next step of their irrevocable evolution together. Nothing could he turn aside.

With me, in the beginning anyway, it was discussions of Yeats or Keats or someone. Pushkin and Kafka, too, impressed him. The latter's diaries had had a very different effect than *The Metamorphosis* and *A Hunger Artist* which we read together. *The Judgment* too, had taken a toll on him. The language had awakened something in him, something that at last his mother had recognized and been frightened by. "Kafka's diaries are too much, man," he said to me again and again. "They're too much. I mean, are they true? Can you hate a father that much? Did the guy ever make it up? How could he live with that man every day? Hey, Tom, maybe he tripped, huh? It's possible ain't it?" Then he would just sit for long minutes in which he scanned a sunken reality whose outline I could not discern.

Adolescence changes its people just as its people regularly seem to threaten the institutions we have contrived to help form these people. The passage of years becomes a wild circle of action and reaction; fantasy and reality; the participants as well as the observers feeling the rising and sinking—"bummers" the young call them. I practically never saw Peter Holden on a rise. Many young people use the expression, "he brings me down." True enough. Peter, quite unlike his older brother with whom he could now barely exchange five words, was bringing me down, and a bit of the world too on top of us both. I had met with him ten to fifteen times, the sessions getting longer and more perplexing. Again and again I heard about his father and the brutal scenes of violence that formed a part of his childhood and young adulthood. At last I called a friend and told him of my own uncontrollable anger and my decision to confront this unseen father who was continuing to cause such hurt. Social science and psychotherapy ethics, as well as political perspectives, could no longer constrain me, I said. There comes a time when one must confront these people and tell them what's happening in the world. There comes a time when one doesn't want to know the reasons behind or the implications of his actions. One merely wants to act. I had convinced myself that this Holden father, who had just about destroyed Johnnie, was for sure going to complete the destruction of Peter. And how many more children were there in that family for him still to devour? Four? Five? I was going to see this man, whatever the consequences, in his own home, on his own time, despite the counseling of my friend to back off. I had heard the words ''overidentification,'' ''countertransference,'' and the ''dangers of upgrading'' too many times. If the man threw me out that would be fine; he had that right. But I would have my say just long enough for him to know that I had feelings that transcend my relationship with his son. He would, at least, have met me.

Now the memories collect themselves. It is an April evening, the Red Sox have just opened the new season at home but the weather seems unsure still. Ominous winter chills refuse to recede but baseball surely will make everything warm again. Five phone calls and we have settled on a time for an appointment; I am frightened. Lots of nice looking girls walking around Cambridge tonight though. Do you suppose lower-class people really are more sexual? Can you imagine if I ever raised that question with the people I know? Amazing how it all becomes a television show. So much of reality itself now, it seems, copies the tube. Pretty soon professionals will arrive from the coast to instruct social scientists and therapists how to *act* with the people with whom they work. But then actors will have to coach the clientele, the patients, the kids, the couples contemplating divorce. Maybe they already do. It's all so crazy. The whole world is crazy. Eight o'clock at night and I'm walking into a darkened neighborhood where people live who have nothing whatsoever in the world in common with me except for one troubled youth who cuts school and comes to see me, and talks poetry. Gerard Manley Hopkins!

Then the apartment building; walking up decaying wooden steps to a freshly painted front door; the inside hall; the names on the mailboxes; the inner door, which surely has not been locked in years, leading to the apartments; the worn rubber treads on the stairs, and the shabby halls. What's the use of describing these scenes anymore?

''That you, Cottle?'' It was *his* voice coming from the very top. That's his voice, eh? Jesus. Thunder had rumbled in the poorly lighted stairwell. That you, Cottle, huh? I felt myself whistling in that breathy way, whisper whistling or whatever it's called. At last I made it to the top, panting a trifle more than I really had to, just to make him believe I was older than I was; out of shape and all that.

''I'm glad to meet you, Mr. Holden,'' I said. ''Fact, I'm just glad to make it up these stairs. You gotta be a young man to negotiate them.'' I smiled. He looked quizzical. I held out my hand. He said, "Yeah," and turned to go inside. We were both shaking our heads. But no matter, for whatever happened I was taller than he was, and men know that that always matters. Moreover, I had been in this home before with Peter, and whether or not Mr. Holden knew this, the fact remained that I had something going with his son and knew my way around. Funny, I remember wondering at the time what it must be like to face the husband of a woman with whom one is having an affair.

"You've been here before so you know where the living room is," he said without looking at me. "I'm going in the kitchen for a beer. You want one?"

"No. No thanks. I just ate and I think I'm set."

"Don't be so polite. Around here you don't have to be so polite. We ain't Harvard here. I'll bring a beer in; maybe you'll change your mind."

Malcolm Holden was a man of average height with a sizable chest and belly, particularly his belly. It was large and taut under the long-sleeved, checkered sport shirt. He wore freshly cleaned beige trousers, shiny loafers, and white socks. His features were small, but his nose and lips were thick. Barely visible pock marks lined the upper rim of his cheeks. I recall going through a list of his characteristics, attempting to match them with my expectations of him. The face was red enough, the arms and neck and belly big enough; the thinning silver hair and hairline just about right, and the quality of his features, actually, not that far off. But those pants! And the loafers and white socks! Indeed, the whole clean appearance. That I hadn't counted on. He had returned with two cans of beer. "You wanna glass?"

"No. Don't need one. This is perfect."

"Who you kidding? You never drink beer from a can unless you wanna impress the old lady. Right?" He laughed the words almost as one reads them in a book. Hah, hah, hah, hah, hah.

"I gotta admit, you're right, Mr. Holden."

"Out of a can, eh?"

"Yeah, I'm sorry. I think I just wanted to make it easier for you."

"Huh?"

"You know, save you the trouble of getting glasses and all."

"Oh." There was a pause.

"I'm really very happy that we could get a chance, maybe, to speak a bit about Peter," I started. Another pause.

"Yeah?"

Listen, you sonofabitch, I thought. Don't you just sit there with that gut of yours, giving out with "hugh's" and "yeah's" and "oh." I didn't come here for that. You won the first round with the beer cans and the glasses routine, but don't forget for a minute that you've lost the other fourteen rounds when it comes to your kids, and to your wife. Man, if this is the kind of shit you hand out to your family on a regular basis, if this is what those family therapist types are used to dealing with, then it's no wonder Peter is . . .

"I've been spending some time talking with him, you know, and I thought we should talk," I heard myself saying. "You and I, that is. Peter didn't suggest it, I want you to know that. I thought it might be a good idea, you know, and that's why I called you."

"You're the guy who did . . . ah . . . with my son John, aren't you." It was not a question.

"Yessir."

"Sent him off to college and all that."

"He's a terrific kid."

"I wouldn't know."

"I don't understand," I said. We were sitting in the living room, I on an old couch facing a bricked-up fireplace painted green to match the wall, Mr. Holden on an easy chair at right angles to me. There was a silence as he sat erect and still, looking at me as though to say, so you're the guy I have to compete with for the *possession* of my sons. So you're the guy. A phoney drinker, phoney panting, overly polite, long-haired intruder who can't even handle an eleven word question: "I'm going in the kitchen for a beer. You want one?" So you're the guy. You'll have to excuse me but I can't believe it.

The even intensity of his staring was preventing me, suddenly, from getting in touch with the anger I was feeling for him. But it was there, along with plenty of other feelings: Hey, Mr. Holden, is this the room where you beat your wife? And is that the table your two little boys had to reset for dinner when you with your violence pulled the dishes off? Where's the bedroom where they had to drag her? And that reminds me, where do you hit Peter? In here, or do you take him into the kitchen or out back somewhere? Do you wear your clean after-work loafers and white socks when you beat him, or do you crack him while you still have on your mud-caked boots which I saw out in the hall? Say, any traces of your wife's blood still on the floor? No, I suppose you can always move some of these throw rugs around to cover up the spots.

I smiled a faint smile, my cheeks feeling like iron weights. "Really, I don't understand. Don't you see Johnnie?"

"*John* and I never speak. That is, not since you and your little friends decided I wasn't doing a good job with him. I mean, not being a *real* father to him. Isn't that about it?"

"No, not really," I replied.

"Then suppose you tell me just exactly what the truth *is.*"

"Well, it's more our feeling that we like to work with kids, like Johnnie, and Peter—"

"Let's leave Peter out of this discussion for a moment, may we," he interrupted. "We'll get to *him* in a minute."

"Well, we feel that quite often schools fail children—" Why can't one tell these people right out what one believes. We hold back, saving it all for the parties and books and seminars. We make all sorts of pledges the night before our

visits but on their ground we're timid, compromising, and always compassionate, so we believe. Maybe in the end, that's the best way.

"They're not children, Doctor, ah, Cottle? Is it Cottle?"

"Yeah. Cottle. Please call me Tom. Yes. Anyway, so when schools don't
have the time to work with some of the kids we try to help out, too. A little bit.
With their work and all."

"But you're a psychiatrist, aren't you?"

"No not really. But I do work with some kids who are having psychological problems." My own words would have made me distrust me. Psychological
problems. Disturbance. Trauma. Countertransference. Mr. Holden just sat there,
immobile. Neither of us had taken a drink.

"You're not a psychiatrist but you work with kids' problems. And who
gives you the permission to do this?" he asked.

"Well, in this case, your wife."

"I see. I see. You mean what the father says doesn't matter any more. The
world belongs to psychiatrists, mothers and kids, eh?"

"Well, I, don't really think . . ."

"You see what I'm saying? You follow me, Doctor?"

"Yessir."

"You don't have to yessir me, son. Save that for Harvard. I've been a
welder's foreman three years here. Pretty young to have that job. I got now
fifteen guys, damn good men, work for me. None of 'em calls me 'Sir.' You
don't have to call me 'Sir.' It's not the words that matter, it's showing respect
and appreciation day by day."

It was becoming a television show. Any minute George C. Scott or one of
those hip lawyers like Joseph Campanella or James Farentino would come out of
the kitchen and take the whole thing over. It wasn't a *déjà vu:* we were playing
out some cliche ridden script. I could practically hear some swish director with a
billowy sleeved shirt and sleazy pants: Now remember, Holden, you're an angry,
bitter man who's lost faith in America and can't really admit it, if in fact he
understands it. You gotta show that pressure, that never-explained tension.
Know what I mean? You're a wife beater, a kid wrecker, you know the type, see
'em every day of your life, yet you believe deep down in your heart you're really
doing the best you can and that guys like Cottle here, good or bad, right or
wrong, have no right interfering in your life. For that matter, they got no business
even being in your home. Okay. Good. Work on it. Now, Cottle, you've come in
with anger to beat the band. So far so good. You know about this guy; you've
gotten the word on him. From social workers, Upward Bound people. Right?
You know him, you know his kind, you know the dangers he presents. Now, you
also know his kid who's the guy you really side with. So in you come with the
anger and the knowledge, but also with a sense of, you know, principle. Ethics,
whatever the hell you want to call it. You know you gotta hold your feelings in
check, but you also gotta let *us* know that something's boiling inside. It's not

working out well. From the beginning you know you're not going to make it. You're losing round after round; pretty soon you're going to lose the whole thing. It's not going to be like those other shows, you know, where justice wins out. The audience has got to see that you're definitely in the right but that you're not going to make it with this guy. Human nature is not gonna change with one confrontation this time. Okay? Got it? Now, show me the tension. No, no, no. Don't, don't grimace. Show the tension with your body. Move around on the couch. Just slightly. Change positions like your back's hurting or something. Use your body. Good. Good. Very good. That's good. Just like that. Don't change a thing. Awright. Let's take it from that second stare. Holden, you're getting ready for the big speech and the revelations. Cottle, you're resigned, getting interested, changing, but still burning inside. Don't forget the body. Holden, you're only going to be effective if you stay real still. Body at right angles, turning the head. A little more. Hold it! Good. Good. Oh, one last thing. Remember, Holden, you're not a heavy. You're a victimized guy, profoundly unhappy, never had enough, and this punk psychologist, who doesn't look the part, wants to throw it all up to you. Okay. Let's try a take. And there was silence on the set.

"Yes, well, Mr. Holden, I want to talk, if we might, a bit about Peter."

"No, we ain't going to talk about Peter because you and Peter are through! You're not seeing him any more."

"I don't understand."

"There's nothing *to* understand. If there's understanding, I'm going to be doing it from now on."

"Is something wrong?" I asked, and felt at once it was the worst question I could have asked.

"Is something wrong? Is that the question? Is something wrong? That's what you want to know? You come into my house when I'm not here and talk poetry with my kid Peter. You send John to a school I've never seen and the kid never writes. I don't know what you did to *him*. I haven't seen him in ten months. What's more, you got it arranged I don't have to pay for the boy. Everything's free. Everything's a scholarship. Money coming in to him from all over God's country, eh? And you expect me to be thankful for taking the burden off my back? Poor man, struggling to keep his family eatin', can't pay for his kid's education. A failure. You arrange for the money just like that, and I'm s'posed to be beholden. Yes? Is something wrong? I'm not your patient, Doctor. And don't you forget that while you're in my house. I'm not one of your boys or one of your freaky playmates in Harvard Square. I don't care how smart they are. I didn't go to college, if you want to know. You probably went to Harvard?"

"Yessir."

"Yeah, well I wasn't as fortunate, shall we say. I'll tell you the truth, I didn't finish high school. I'm not ashamed to say it. Went second year and quit. Oh, don't get me wrong," he went on ironically, "we loved all the subjects and all the teachers. The teachers, especially, they were wonderful. They were so wonderful and understanding. Not like today. I mean they just said, like, 'Malcolm you didn't do your little homework, so naughty, naughty. Try to do better tomorrow.' '' I tried my best to smile but the invisible weights on my cheeks were even heavier than before. His tone changed. "Would you like to know what they did in those days? They did exactly what my father did. They cracked you in the side of the head when you didn't shape up and told you to do the work or get the hell out. They screamed at you and embarrassed you before your friends in the class. My God how they embarrassed us! You wouldn't know about that. You're too young. How old are you, anyway, that you're suddenly taking over for all the crummy fathers and school teachers in the world? What, about thirty maybe. Less? Huh?''

"Hmm. Yes. I do know something about the schools you're describing though. Not everything's that different. You should visit some of—''

"What do you know? What are you talking about? The schools haven't changed? You ask your father what schools were like when he went. Your father living?''

"Yes.''

"He work?''

"Yes.''

"What does he do?''

"He's a doctor.''

"A doctor? A doctor like you or a doctor?''

"A doctor. Surgeon.''

"Some guy I'm asking about schools. Millionaire's son.'' He looked toward the hall as though he were speaking to someone.

"We're not exactly millionaires,'' I said.

"Your father's a millionaire all right,'' he responded abruptly. "He's a millionaire. Don't forget, son, some people call themselves by what they earn in a year. Like your father. Other guys have to call themselves by what they earn in a lifetime. I work just as hard as your father and will never make anywhere near as much as he does. I'll bet his house doesn't look like this. Huh? Tell me, does it?''

"Well, there are some similar—''

"Come off it.''

"Well, no.'' Okay, you're right, but don't call me ''son.''

"Well no,'' the man says. "And you drink beer, do you, you and your father, out of a can every night?''

"No. We don't.''

"And your father, this is great, your father, tell me, has psychiatrists or psychologists or cheap-looking college kids coming to his house in the evening or calling him five times a week to set up an appointment to talk with him about his son?''

"No. That's never happened.'' Jesus, God Almighty. His voice suddenly was beginning to crack and get so old-sounding. What if he started to cry, maybe drop dead right on the spot? Oh my God. My few words were so soft.

"You follow me?" Mr. Holden asked.

"Yes, I do."

"You see, there's a big difference, isn't there?" he said.

"Yes," I obeyed, "there's a difference."

"Well, that's the reason you and Peter are finished. No more messing around or whatever you two do together. I may be the world's worst father but I'm still a man and the boy's father, and I'm not about to turn him over to you. Not this time. You got one, okay, but I'm keeping this one. I don't care what happens to him. You don't have to stick your nose into it. You don't have to call me five times every week. Call someone else for a change." Then, for no reason, neither of us spoke for several minutes.

"I want you, Doctor, to put yourself into my shoes." At last, as a page somewhere turned and his tone softened, I felt a spell of relief. "Fact is, I'd like for you to spend a day or two with me. Huh? How 'bout it? Come down to the shop. Meet the boys. Eat where we eat. Go drinking a little, you know. You like it? Surely Harvard guys drink." He was excited by his own suggestion. Beer out of a can, I thought. Real cute. "You come with me. The whole day, like. Forget the youngsters for a while. Let 'em go one day. Look at the older generation just a little for a change. Take a little vacation. Peter says you do a little writing, eh?"

"A little," I responded.

"About people, like? About real life?"

"Yes, about people. Real life, I guess."

"Good. Hey, maybe you could write a little story about us. You know, at the shop, after work, at the bar. Human interest stuff. What they call a slice of life. That'd be good, wouldn't it? It's a good thought, ain't it? You know what I mean? You don't see stuff about my kind very often. I read the *Traveler* and *Globe* pretty regular. You never see a piece in those Sunday magazines about fathers, or just plain working men. No one gives a hoot about us. Cops, maybe, or what they're callin' the hardhats every once in a while. You could do it. A first. Maybe you could get famous or something."

"I'd like to try." Try what? I mused. To write the story of this man or get famous?

"Did you ever write about fathers? I'll bet you never did. Did you?"

All right, all right, don't rub it in. Mr. Holden, do you know, I mean, is it possible that you could have found out about my imagined diatribe against you? Did I say something by mistake tonight? . . . "No, I never have. It's a good idea." He was right. A day in the life of Ivan Denisovich in East Cambridge. It would be like those British writers describing the miners in Northern England. He was right. His side *is* forgotten. All those social worker reports I had read had always made me assume that the father of some "disturbed" youngster was either absent or a drunk, or was sick or dumb or something vile. Fathers were in fact "things." We never even saw "the father" unless a male social worker was lucky enough to snare him for an afternoon. Who talks to all these guys anyway? In the hospitals it's usually the mothers who bring the frightened child onto the ward. Who does care about fathers even in this time of sustained male supremacy? James Agree did. He spoke about fathers. So did William Faulkner. And so does Robert Coles. Holden, I've changed my mind. Your idea's not so hot. There have been books written on your kind, I mean, about fathers having a tough time and all. Don't think you have any monopoly on oppression and victimization. You don't own powerlessness, you know. So don't *you* forget that!

"Yeah. It's a good idea, ain't it?" Mr. Holden was continuing. "You come down and I'll show you what it's like to work a ten-hour day, and why it is that maybe a guy would like to have a beer or two before he comes home, night after night after night." His anger was building again, but his words seemed utterly coherent. His voice no longer sounded weak, and his body, which moved so slightly as he spoke, had become strong again. He was a postoperative open heart case rebounding. The unseen director's admonitions were being followed exactly. I didn't grimace. Nor did I smile. I did move with subtle difficulty on the couch, however. It was partly real, partly acted. Malcolm Holden was holding forth. All the fathers in the neighborhood were holding forth, and winning. Every round now, every fight, the preliminaries and the main event. Malcolm Holden was not about to cry, nor would he die of a broken heart or some cerebral arterial explosion as I had imagined—as once I might have wished.

At least once, someone should tell me about older men and younger men together; about authority relations and what ultimately constitutes the bonds that keep a leader and his followers together. Just once, someone should explain how I could be placed in the position of being a son to this man so unlike my own father, in this house so unlike any home I had known or ever would know. Why then, was I being urged into the role of son with him? I never felt like a father to his sons, or any young people for that matter. So why then does the man on the bottom have to submit to this psychological trap, to this primitive inevitability? Think, for example, of what we learned to say as children when someone our age or barely older was punishing us, making us yield to his indefatigable strength and self-proclaimed domination. "Uncle," we would scream, or "Kings. Kings. Kings. Please, please let me up. I'll do whatever you want me to but you're hurting my arm. I swear, I'll do what you want. Please!" We would be crying by then. And the kid, whoever he was, would wait that trying, cruel wait, and let us up, but not before he caused one last pain that might make the torture permanent.

"I want you to know *me*, not my sons," Malcolm Holden was saying. "Anybody ever do research on guys like me? All you care about is the kids, probably 'cause they have a *future*. What the hell I got left anyway? August twenty-eighth I'm going to be forty-four years old. That seem old to you, Doctor? Forty-four?"

"No. Not really."

"No? I ain't no spring chicken, you know. Neither's the old lady. I got a little ways to go before retirement, although to hear these kids around here talk about it you'd think I was ready for a hospital or old lady's home already. My father died when he was twenty-four. He was one of those builders, you know, builds high buildings and bridges. Steel worker is what he was. Got crushed to death. I barely knew him. Fact is, I can't even remember him. The old lady didn't have a single picture of him. She just threw him out of her memory like you'd rip a page out of the phone book. You know what I mean?"

"Yes."

"Yup. One down and God only knows how many to go for her. We had more men coming in and out of our house as a boy. 'This is your Uncle This or Uncle That,' she'd say. Who the hell was she trying to kid, I wonder. Christ, we'd see 'em together in the room at night taking off their clothes and humpin' the shit out of each other. We had a place half this size then. Kids slept in the big room, five of us. I had a kid sister died right after she was born, too. Nobody knows to this day who *her* father was. Died so soon nobody even found a name for her. Never had a name. Think of *that*. Jesus. Anyway, we slept in this big room and she slept in the one bedroom. Didn't even bother to close the door most of the time. Then when I was about six, she marries this guy Holden, and we all have to change our name and ways and everything. She had a lot of nerve, my mother. She comes in the house one night drunk as a goddamn lord and says, 'Now you listen to me for once. This is your new father,' she goes. 'I want everyone to love him as I do and respect him and do whatever he says in the house.' God, I will *never* forget that scene if I live to be a hundred years old. Love him and respect him, and the two of them there can barely stand up in front of us, laughin' and all. Just 'cause you're a kid, you know, doesn't mean you forget that kind of thing. You know what I mean?" I couldn't answer him. I sat there, motionless, watching him intently, using my senses to flush respect and compassion into my face. He was in a melancholy reverie, his being draped in the blankets of his childhood, his senses working to blow away the dust that clings to the surfaces of the events and people that constitute history.

"You know, I can still see them. And every time I think of that evening . . . it was a Tuesday. For some reason I always remember it as a Tuesday. Like tonight. That's funny, ain't it? I still see them. The two of 'em. One minute I have no father and I'm Malcolm Henry Savanola. The next minute I got a father again and I'm Holden. I mean, just like that. My brother Henry, 'Henkie' we used to call him, God bless him, he passed away this time two years ago. Terrible. Forty he was. Just turning forty. They found a cancer, right here at City Hospital, and he was gone. Bingo." He snapped his fingers. "Just like that. God bless him. One minute he was with us, the next minute he was gone. Strangest damn thing I ever saw. Absolutely healthy, big and strong like an ox. Then, poof. He was gone.'' Mr. Holden halted momentarily for something to pass.

"Anyway, I remember 'Henkie' standing there holding Margaret's hand, that's my older sister. He says to my old lady: 'What should we call him? Still Uncle Robert?' That was his name. Robert. Can you beat that? 'Still uncle,' he goes. God strike me dead if that isn't exactly what he said. One minute that sonofabitch is a friend from business, or an uncle or somethin', and the next minute he's our father. I'll never forgive him that. He wasn't well a day in his life in that house. And we had to wait on him. Jesus, how I hated that. The girls didn't mind it that much. He just barely had the strength to get out of bed once or twice a day to take a crap or yell at us. Or beat the crap out of us more likely. And she let him, like we were his kids, not hers. Fact is, when he didn't have the energy, *she'd* take to beating us. I remember times for no good reason, she'd just come up to us where we'd be playin' or something, and *boom*.'' He pounded his right fist into the palm of his left hand. "We didn't know a moment of peace. Not in that house or at school. Nowhere. We were always talkin' about running away somewhere. There was always a fight or an argument. Jesus Christ, that unnamed sister, I told you, wasn't buried two hours we came home fighting about something or other. There was always someone being hit. Always. It was always the same. Every day.'' His voice trailed off.

"I never really told the story of my life to anyone.'' He looked at me, expecting something, asking something perhaps. I nodded. "I'm not sure what I want of you. I don't know what I'd like you to say. Maybe before I did. Lotta people have had it tough. Maybe what I'm doing is feelin' sorry for myself or making a whole lot of excuses. Who knows? Maybe that's what I'm doing. Maybe fathers are tough on their kids. Maybe especially on their sons. What do you think? Maybe I'm right, huh? But I just didn't know any other way. When a kid got out of line, you hit him. That's what I grew up on, like pablum. That's what I learned, and that's what I passed on. Kid's got to show respect for his elders, particularly his father. That's the basis of the family. He doesn't have to love 'em. I didn't love my old man, I mean, you know, my stepfather. I never really knew what kind of a man my real father was. But this guy Holden, him I knew. I was glad when they both died. I mean it, even if God's listening to me right now. I hated them. I wanted them both dead, my mother and my stepfather. It was the only thing that coulda stopped them. Then, when my own Johnnie was born, I sort of went crazy you could almost say. In the beginning it was okay 'cause Mary, my wife, did most all the work. But when he got older and the other kids came along I'd lose my temper all the time and hit him or run out of the house or go find the boys and have a drink. The bills began piling up. You borrow up to here, if you can even get the credit. You can't take vacations like guys you hear about. You work two, maybe three jobs. Maybe you get one afternoon a week free, like Sunday maybe, and the kids are running around making noise. And the place is too small for everybody.

"What's the use.'' He blew out a long breath. "What's the use any more.'' I made a gesture to leave. It was an ambiguous motion but he held his hand out to detain me. "Stay one minute. I want to tell you one more thing. Like a confession, you know what I mean, Doctor?" He laughed quietly.

"Yes, I do."

"I've fooled around a bit. You know what I mean? You know, a woman here and there. I can't say that I've been totally faithful. I'll be truthful. In the beginning I was. That's the God's truth. Then the kids came and like I said, something happened. Like, especially when she'd be pregnant. I'd have a few drinks in a bar like at Carmen's, or someplace, and meet someone, and, you know. But I swear to you, I was always discreet and proper. I never let on. No one ever found *me* anywhere with a woman, you know, like with a door open somewhere, or running around half-naked in front of a bunch of kids. I never told no one. And I never loved these women what's more. Nah. I see one from time to time still. I'll tell you that. It doesn't bother me that much to say this. I see one regular like. I don't love her. Nothing like that. I know what I see her for and she does too. We don't make any lies to one another. You just come to expect things from certain people. I never made it out to be any more than it was. I'd get a feeling, you know, and go on over to Carmen's. Maybe I'd find someone and score, maybe not. It was never that serious to me. But you know how it is, you can't spend every night of your life the same way, in front of the television with a can of beer—or a glass." He looked at me and smiled for the first time. He *did* like me. Suddenly, we were boxers after a fight; weary boxers with our gloves removed, our hands still taped, our bodies hurting, hugging each other after the last bell, thankful to have survived, and waiting for the decision and for tomorrow's pain. I wanted to reach out and touch him. Not a mere handshake. Maybe to slap his back or clutch the upper part of his arm. Maybe a clinch or a hug. Maybe there would be no decision after all. Maybe they would give the championship crown and diamond studded belt to both of us; equal fame to the older man and the younger man. Had we shaken hands when I arrived? I think not. No, we hadn't.

"I just wanted to let you know some things. I'm sorry to take your time. I know you have to go." Mr. Holden had uttered the words but either one of us might have said them. "I did want you to know a little about *me*. Maybe understand me. Maybe it will help with your work. Say, maybe you *could* come down and see where I work. You know much about metal work? Huh?" He turned toward me.

"No. Not much, I'm afraid." I spoke more freely than before. Words that earlier were heard as condescending might now be construed as endearing, perhaps even naïve and charming.

"Know anything about metal work at all, Doctor?" he repeated.

"No. I can't say that I do." From an inner resource somewhere, masculinity was crawling back into my body. "We lived near Gary when I was a boy, so I used to see the mills all the time, but I never really did understand what was happening there."

"Well, Gary. That's the big time already. What they got there," he thought aloud, ''Inland, Bethlehem, U.S.—that's what you'd call the major leagues. We're only a small outfit here. But I can still teach you a thing or two about steel. You see if I can't. Try me.''

''You won't embarrass me in front of the class if I don't know the answers?''

He laughed. ''Nope. Schools are different now. I know. A guy who should know told me so.'' We looked at each other. ''You think maybe I tried to clear myself for what I did to John and Peter?'' He was soft again.

''Maybe. I don't know.''

''Yeah. Maybe. Maybe I did. I could have spent a helluva lot more time with them and been more patient probably. Not sent 'em out of the house when I did. But goddammit,'' his anger was on the rise, ''no one ever gave *me* a second look. No one felt sorry for *me*. I was, like, doomed from the start. Nothing I did seemed to be any good to anyone. D'you know the feeling of being a failure? Of lying to yourself that what you got for an entire lifetime of work doesn't even matter at all? I know I'm not foolin' anyone. I got men working for me, like I say. Sure, fifteen of 'em, but I've had hundreds of men I got to account to all the time. Still do, even today as a foreman, forty-four years old. My whole life it's been the same thing. You make one slip and you're out of a job. That's the way it is, like it or not. You know what that means? One slip and out of a job? Or maybe some bright guy like you from Harvard or M.I.T. one day is going to invent some goddamn machine, you know, computer, run you right out of work. Boy, I think about *that* every day of my life. I got a lot of friends told me, just like that, they were being replaced or knocked out of business. I don't care what they say or what you read. You get knocked out of a job at my age and you don't just bounce right back in a minute. You know what I mean? Best you can do most of the time is become a bank guard or night watchman or something for half the pay. And that's if you're lucky.'' He didn't wait for a response.

''So you tell *me* how a man's supposed to make it all come together; the bills and the food and maybe then college for a kid or two, even with the scholarships. You tell me what life is supposed to be like, all these goddamn phoney politicians bullshittin' this and that about the common man, the working man, the *struggling* man in the factories, in the inner cities. You know what we get from those bullshitters? Campaign promises, inflation, and unemployment!

''I'll tell you one thing you did for me, Doctor, I'll thank you for it, too. You kept John out of the army for a while. Let him go to school. I'll thank you for that. I served. I did my time. Two years ago, maybe even last year I'd have stepped in and told you all where to go. Let my kids serve in the army, I'd have said. I knew what you were up to. Let 'em do their time. They're going in the army. Men have to go into the army. That's the way it is and should be. But not this war, mister. Not this time. I'll agree with your students this one time. They're right. I don't want my son getting his head blown off in Vietnam or

Cambodia or wherever the hell they are where they shouldn't be no more. For that one thing I'll thank you.''

And I, reflexively, blurted out, ''You're welcome.''

Within minutes, our visit had concluded. We had fumbled through those routinized exchanges about getting together soon, maybe taking a trip to his plant, enjoying the conversation, about how it is always nice to see the face behind the voice, and how the ''results'' of the evening had been so unexpected. Both of us were embarrassed. Both of us had more than merely sparred with guilt and shamefulness. We had had our pride cut into, only to have it heal over quickly, then reappear uplifted, yielding something slightly better than before. Yet, despite the confessions, and the tension and the other ingredients that make what we dryly call human interactions come alive, both of us had avoided something as significant as a single life, something as portentous as the fate of that life.

I avoided it, I confessed to myself outside in the cool night. I ran like hell from it. He's had it tough, that man. God. He should only know what thoughts I've had about him. Maybe someday I'll write the whole thing up and present it to him. It'll be *my* confession, my gift to him. That wasn't easy what he did in there . . . Why didn't I drive? . . . What do those boys over there in the dark want? . . . It wasn't easy. Nobody's life is easy. It never is . . . Jesus, they gotta lotta girls around here and those kids over there are going to get 'em all. And I have to walk through here suave and disinterested like always.

He *is* right though. No one really cares about his life. I don't, at least I didn't two hours ago. I don't even think that much about his side of the story when I'm working with his own boy. I'm won over to the kid's side. Ten words, a little sniffling, some poetry and he's got me, a friend forever. And if the kid reads Kafka . . . He's right. Father dying and a drunken mother, and a sister who dies, and a brother who dies. Rotten stepfather. The man can't even keep his own name. And there's the work threat and being broke. What do the people around the University know about that? Eight, ten blocks away, that stuff's going on, and over here the students are studying or tripping or screwing or going to the movies, and the Cambridge weeknight cocktail parties, and affairs and committee meetings are in full swing, or people are reading their books and magazines. I *should* do a piece on him.

Ach, it's all too cornball, and so hard to know my own feelings. Maybe I'm glad somehow that a lot of people aren't doing what I do. I need these others, the Cambridge cocktail set and the students, to do what they're doing so that I can be somehow, special for what I do. Not brave, exactly, but good, or special.

What in God's name is it? The man's been victimized and I'm ashamed. But a lot of people have it tough. My dad had it tough. And goddammit I have it tough too. I mean, just 'cause you've had these horror stories fall on your head doesn't give you the right to take it out on your kids. Granted, we talk about generational problems and never once for a moment ever think that parents have experienced problems with their parents. We're sucked into young people's visions and interpretations. Well, Erikson and some of the others weren't, but for the most part, we fall into that. I know we do. Or we'll think about people repeating patterns of their childhoods in the most complicated ways, like beating a son because a stepfather's not around to get it, that is, if one had the psychological equipment to attack one's father, the most recent husband of one's mother—not to mention her, that sacred, unblemished beauty. Yet, when we get into the action, when the discussions blaze, just two generations appear before us, and we seem to side with one against the other, or just make believe generational transactions take place in one direction only. Still, it doesn't give the guy the right to ruin his sons. That right he doesn't possess.

What's really going on here? This is a guy who's had it rough and I'm seeing his kid, once, twice a week maybe. And this bitter, moody fourteen-year-old boy who gets his insides beaten out of him practically every month is reading Keats and Yeats and Pushkin and Kafka. And probably because of those fascists who torment him, or a father and a mother, and somehow his grandparents too, who have brutalized him, he's injecting himself with thirty bags of heroin a day. I didn't even know about this until a few weeks ago, and nobody can get this boy to change, or to see someone who might be able to help him. So what happens? His mother finally realizes he is suddenly quiet and withdrawn. I talk to his father and we don't even mention the drug business. We don't even mention *the* problem. I don't even know if the father knows, or if he knows that I know. Or what his mother knows or senses. Or for that matter, what the boy knows. And still, they all love one another and need one another desperately. It's absolutely unbelievable what's going on here.

Conclusion

We commence our concluding remarks with a word of caution. One typically looks to the last chapter of a book to find the ultimate conclusions—the meaning, really, of all that has gone on. But let us recall our reference to this precarious task in the introduction. For there to be final conclusions, conclusive overreaching statements, one has to subscribe to the notion that a phenomenon like the relationship between fathers and sons allows one to draw out universal facts. That is, the ultimately conclusive statement, in this instance, would seem to draw out all the material from the life studies, and lift them into some comprehensive set of notions or constructs meant to satisfy the person eager to know how all these variegated stories fit together as one.

In my own case, I find this sort of task difficult, if not impossible, for, as I stated in the introduction, I am not always certain that universal truths are there for the taking or deducing. Do we perhaps select or obtain bits of information in order to fit them into a mold we then call a universal, or even less extremely, a reasonable conclusion? So, one might do as well hunting for major themes that directly or indirectly run through the various accounts. Let us begin with one of these, namely, the theme described by the concept of generation. A point to be stressed is the effect on a man's association with his son of the power of generations. It is not necessarily the case that fathers raise their sons according to the way their fathers raised them. It is also not necessarily true that fathers raise their sons to do things and reach levels of success or achievement that they were never able to do or attain. Would that it were all so simple. Still, with all of the complexity, the power of generational differences remain. What that means is that no father, irrespective of how in touch he may be with the ongoing currents, trends, and values of the contemporary generation, can fully divorce himself from the generation in which he grew up. That is, a father can never shed the reality that the past was encouched in the currents, trends, and values of another generation, which meant other people, other issues, other events. In a sense, the asymmetry of the relationship is borne with this generational strain: The son knows but one generation, the father two. It often goes under the name of experience, but if fathers have difficulty understanding or appreciating the times in which their sons grow up, sons often have a tendency to explore only minimally the times in which their fathers grew up. Indeed, many boys find the scenes of their fathers' childhood to be almost illicit, if not titillating.

One can look at the matter from another perspective. The birth of children has as one of its significant by-products the creation of a set of experiences sociologists call *generational continuity*. For some people the flow of time, the emergence of history—if one can properly use this phrase—is little more than the flow of family members, one generation to the next. Life itself is affirmed, along with the idea of being alive when one's children are born and one feels there is now some legacy, some continuity. We tend to oversimplify this point when we say rather derisively that what *all* people want out of their children is to perpetuate their own names, or their family names, or even their own personal traditions. Granted, some people probably do enjoy the idea that they can achieve immortality—and thereby trick time, as it were—by having, typically, their sons "carry on" for them. Granted, too, many fathers presumably view their sons, especially, as little more than appendages or narcissistic reflections of themselves. But in assuming these perspectives, we tend to overlook a more universal phenomenon cultivated in and through the dynamics of generational strain and intimacy.

One of the most terrifying and dreadful human sensations is that of feeling helpless. The culture surely holds up independence and autonomy as ideals for children, probably, still, male children in particular, just as it shuns the notion that people should ever feel dependencies. Dependency depicts weakness, the lack of self-sufficiency, industriousness. It probably even denotes effeminacy in some men's minds. Ideals or not, the point is that everyone by the laws of human nature is dependent on other people. Indeed, the shunning of dependency speaks not to human truths at all, but quite likely to that more terrifying feeling, the dread of being helpless. Surely the sensation of helplessness commences in infancy. Without a parent, we die. For that matter—and how many adolescents decry this point—if it weren't for a couple of parents we wouldn't even *be* here. We wouldn't be! So our very being in the world *depends* on the existence not only of two other people, but of the dynamic power of generations enduring. The expression of taking over the reins is an apt one. When people are old enough, they take over for their parents—at least they do in agricultural societies where it is expected that the son merely follow in his father's footsteps. In industrial cultures this matter of taking over the reins is diminished, if not made altogether invisible. That a father may *wish* to pass the reins on does not guarantee him that the opportunity to do so may eventually arise. But notice here, where the reins go free—and the metaphor seems to grow in appropriateness—the son in effect is asking to lead his life on his own, no matter how terrifying the lack of his father's help may be to him.

Ironically, given all the expressions of generational strain and intimacy inherent in the father–son association, it is traditionally the mother in the family who protects the son from experiencing the pains of helplessness. In many families, in other words, the impress of the father on the child only begins when the father believes the son is old enough to make it on his own, which means not crumble at the first trial at self-sufficiency. In this regard, it could be said that the father introduces the son if not exactly to the outside world, then at least to the feelings and belif systems that one must adopt and honor when dealing with the outside world—which means the world apart from the mother. But note again, both the mother and father offer to or impose on the child a far more complex message and mission than that described by their individual personalities. In fact the substance and power of generational continuity is being impressed on the child. The living and lived experiences of an entire generation play their roles in the shaping of the child's sense of his or her identity and aspirations. So by definition we may be obliged to ''study'' a boy and his father, or a man and his father, but if those universals we speak of are to be delineated, then we must assume that any father–son association has been shaped in part by the individual as well as collective evolution of entire human groups. Let us attempt to make the argument more concrete.

When a man tells his son, or feels, that there are some special paternal tasks that he must undertake, isn't he in fact addressing matters associated with the generic definition of being a father? That is, his definition of the role, if he uses that word, or some inchoate sense of fathering, fatherness or fatherhood, are hardly drawn from out of the blue. Nor are they entirely described by the way his father raised him. Cultures shape the definitions of the father–son association; societies do as well, not to mention the numerous institutions that also speak to the manner in which sons and fathers must relate to one or another, or define those qualities constituting their relationship. Surely each man wishes to find and treasure the idiosyncratic aspects of his relationship with his son; he wants it to be special, *unique*. But the uniqueness draws its life from the universal truths governing this one bond. That is what is meant by the capacity to deal not merely with the abstract term ''fatherhood,'' but to deal with the historical emergence within a culture of this precious relationship. In practical terms, the notion of fatherness, or fatherhood, is made understandable in part by the evolution of generations and the completeness or felt sense of this evolution that a man feels when his children are born. The chain is not complete, a father senses, until the next link is born.

A word of disclaimer. We are not suggesting that only men, or men who become fathers, feel this linkage, this set of connections between generations; we are only suggesting that the father–son association is in part influenced not only by the impact of the individual personalities involved, but by the nature of the entire dynamic movement known as "generational continuity." A father and son encounter one another. But their encounter encompasses the nature of father-ness meeting son-ness. Thus, whole generations are conjoined in this encounter, despite the fact that the two principals involved feel and define the encounter in wholly different terms. Not only that; as time passes, they will continue to rearrange and recontextualize their feelings about and definitions of the encounter. But let use pursue the temporal nature of the encounter one step further.

By definition, the father has experienced a form of what the son is or will experience. Let us say, both know analogous experiences. In some cases even, a father works hard, consciously or unconsciously, to make certain that his son goes through experiences analogous to what he, the father, once went through. We might even allege, in this argument, that some men treat the father–son association as if it were a sacred club and hence choose to initiate their son "into the club." While this particular metaphor may seem foreign to some people, an examination of certain fraternities and fraternal orders would support the notion. After all, any initiation ceremony has its subordinate and superordinate memberships opposing one another, with the purpose of the initiation being a test of the initiate's *manhood*. To be allowed entrance into the club, the membership or the order as it is often called constructs an iniation—a procedure carried out in a variety of ways in numerous cultures. But note always the symbolism: The older one and the younger one; the experienced one and the inexperienced one; the older one hoping the younger one will "make it" but realizing making it implies *on one's own*. And if there is ever doubt about the initiation ceremony, the father-like figures can always allege, we are asking nothing of you that we ourselves have not already experienced.

Manhood seems to be at stake in most of these club-like ceremonies: surviving with grace and competence when put to the test. It is the man's job, it would seem, to bring the child out of boyhood into manhood. Besides being a temporal act in character, the transition reveals its sexual overtones as well, for is not boyhood associated with the mother and hence femininity. Manhood means not needing mommy any more, which is further intended to mean, not needing *anyone* but oneself. If it weren't a man's job to get his son beyond the (weakening and cheapening) dependencies of childhood, why else would all these initiation to manhood ceremonies so assiduously exclude women? Clearly, there are just some things, often of a secretive nature, that men must do together. We see this secretive, almost primordial, character in many of the preceding life studies. In a few instances, one senses that its foundation may be the biological alliance that men only naturally form. I am like daddy, not like mommy, the male child decides. True enough, the biological, or at least anatomical differences are what keep the boys from the girls, or more precisely in psychological terms, the boys from becoming girls. But traditionally, fathers must make certain that the anatomical distinction is not the only feature that legitimates a separation or a differentiation of a boy from his sisters or girls in general. For this job, women simply have been denied.

If we combine these points, we notice another theme heard throughout various accounts: namely that fathers do far more, consciously and unconsciously, than live out the unhappy or ungratified moments of their own lives. Granted, the characterization of the father pushing his son to fill the voids of his, the father's, life finds confirmation in certain life histories. But to argue that this is the dominant mode of the father–son association is to assume the position that father–son relationships are essentially predicated on the father's psychopathological personality. One can just as rightly allege that fathers struggle with the task of leading their lives partly to prepare for the future of their son's lives. More generally, many parents assume this responsibility for their children. Nonetheless, the point to be stressed is the distinction between being a bridge between the generations, on the one hand, and having one's child's world be compensation for one's own felt inadequacies, on the other. This is not to say, however, that many fathers, as some of the preceding accounts reveal, feel no ambivalence about their role. More than one father in the course of history has muttered about the sacrifices he has made for his sons. Still, sacrifice and compensation are hardly of the same psychological character. Furthermore, they bespeak different sociological orientations to the role of father and son.

In great measure, the accounts we have heard allow us to examine the theme of the father laying ground work for the son. We have also heard fathers recount the sort of life preparation laid for them by their own fathers. In part the preparation is real. Tangible, practical matters are solved by the father, just as decisions are made for him. In this regard, it is almost laughable to think that children must mature to the point where they make momentous life decisions when so many momentous life decisions have already been made for them.

We stress this point because of the significance of the concept of autonomy. The father, it is said, is the prime teacher for the son if only because it is the father's role to assist the son in the young man's growth toward a self-governing approach to life. Not surprisingly, this self-governing dynamic requires that the son lean heavily, if not feel utterly dependent, on his father. But in traditional terms, it seems to be the father's job to convince the son that dependency simply cannot be considered an acceptable posture. As I mentioned earlier, the dependency aspect of the association probably assumes importance because men, generally, face the problem of reconciling their dependencies on each other as well as on women. Why men seem to be so utterly preoccupied with self-government, self-rule, stems perhaps from the fact that neither of their parents has allowed dependency for too long. The irony of all this, of course, is that autonomy, personal self-government, is an utterly unattainable ideal. The model of self-governing nation states is a lovely one for the individual personality to follow. Perhaps the Greeks in their conceptions of democracy set an even loftier example than western culture has ever realized. But individual autonomy in this self-governing fashion may not be an appropriate ideal.

For one thing, there is far too much ambivalence associated with it. People ultimately rely on a host of other people, whether or not they wish to acknowledge it. Similarly, they have come to depend on their parents with far greater intensity than they may wish to acknowledge. Surely this point comes across in many of the life studies. We have also heard of some of the genuine difficulties one faces in becoming what we still call the self-made man. Typically, "self-made" implies that one has received little or no help from one's father. But if the life studies teach us one thing, it is that no son honestly believes he goes through life untouched, unaided by his father. The mere biological fact of the predecessor, the progenitor, seems to strike each of the men examined as sufficient evidence for the fact that they are not, in some deeply existential sense, self-made. This point takes us into what might be considered a spiritual aspect of the father–son association.

Fathers and sons, if their encounters can be called spiritual, must find in each other, or more precisely *sense* in each other, the notion of the mystery, or the mysterious. That they share the same gender ties them together in some atavistic fashion. That they are of the same flesh and blood—a metaphor the Bible underwrites so frequently—further affirms this attachment. But there is something else. Do we call it destiny, time, the miracle of life perpetuating life? Do we call it generational succession, human inheritance, the flow of one family to the next? Whatever it means to us, fathers and sons are united in a spiritual way; they are the living representatives, the closest approximations, of one another's pasts and futures. It is within this context that one finds the living power of words like ambition, self-made man, success, and failure. At some point in all our lives, we must wonder about the more comprehensive scheme of existence. What does it mean to be alive. What does it mean to say *I am alive*. What is the connection of my life to others' lives, and especially those significant others' lives, like my parents and my children. Quite probably these questions are not addressed until people in biological, spiritual, or philosophical terms are able to appreciate the literal and symbolic association of parent and child, and one suspects in our culture, father and son.

The attachment to living may be for the son, the father; that is, until his own son is born. The attachment moreover to the transcendent, the spiritual, may again be through this association. When we speak about the father–son association, therefore, it may well be that the sacred symbol in fact is the hyphen, the connection of these two human units in time. When we speak of a father who lives out his own life through his son's life, we may jump immediately to the notion of psychopathology. But we can jump as easily to the notion that fathers and sons *are* attached to one another as well as to life itself, and hence an accomplishment by a son is in spiritual if not in psychological terms an accomplishment of the father. Said less extremely, a father's deed is automatically a son's reward, just as a father's loss becomes his son's burden. It is true not because they are one and the same people, but because they are joined spiritually, and thus experience, in one form or another, the burdens and gratifications of each other's lives.

Following this line of thought, and something else one hears in the preceding accounts, the concept of guilt takes on a slightly new meaning. Granted, sons and fathers alike feel guilty about acts committed in the context of their relationship. To be sure, fathers and sons feel guilt stemming from thoughts never uttered within the context of their relationship. If one may say so, these are the profane faces of guilt, as pernicious as they may be. The sacred or spiritual faces of guilt may derive from the existential force to feel that one is autonomous when one must "know" the unbreakable atavistic attachment to one's successors and progenitors. More specifically, one is not made guilty by the mere act of being alive, but more likely by the notion that autonomy, self-government, independence are in fact human transgressions from the just and real nature of the father–son bond. The literal and symbolic nature of the encounter gives birth to a sense of guilt, then, that one cannot believe in the very notion of independence and self-sufficiency when one is forever dependent on other lives for giving biological, philosophical, social, and ultimately spiritual meaning to one's own existence. But let me add one more piece to this rather mysterious puzzle.

In many of the accounts heard in this book, we note the instance of a father wishing he may have had the courage to do what his father or son had done. Or perhaps a particular man hopes his son will dare to confront aspects of reality he was unable to confront. This theme might be labeled the need for a living or existential courage. But notice too the capacity of many of the men to speak of the courage required in recognizing how much one's individual life is caught up in the realm of other lives, shaped in part by these other lives, such that one life draws its strength from the other. Said differently, if it takes courage "merely" to be, it takes courage to be attached, associated with those persons attached not by reason of the will. Fathers and sons do not choose one another; they are *given* or *delivered* to one another. For want of a better phrase, it is an act of God or biological chance that they are obliged to encounter one another. Whereas adolescence is in part characterized by the expression of a courage to stand alone, make it on one's own, adulthood is in part characterized by the willingness to accept encounters, marriages, interdependencies, human associations for the life-affirming bonds that they represent. Ironically, one states that an act of courage is expressed in the willingness to love someone other than oneself.

Common speech contains the phrase, "One cannot love another until one loves oneself." In our adolescent years we "work" at this matter of self-love. (We do a bit of playing at it as well.) In realistic terms, the capacity to love another derives from the experiences of having been loved. We love another only after we have been loved, or, more precisely, after we have participated in encounters born in moments of utter helplessness. Self-love, therefore, is an intermediate process between having been loved and finding the courage to love. In traditional terms—although this now is changing—it was the father's fate to encounter his son only after the son had been the recipient of his mother's love. Fathers did not enter the realm of love teaching, but chose for themselves, instead, the role of teaching the son how to deal with the external world. Respect, obedience, adulation were far more appropriate ideals for the son than love for or intimacy with the father. The encounter, one might say, was built on agentic rather than communal terms. There were real things to be taught, not merely feelings to be felt; and every moment counted. But the feelings were there, no matter how disguised, no matter how deeply and assiduously repressed. About this fact, too, sons experienced guilt. So did many of their fathers. Feelings for one's father are always "there," even if one is never certain just who his father may be.

What makes the father–son relationship complex is that ontogenetic root of the association. One develops in one's mother's womb. Irrespective of how this fact gets confused in the child's mind, the father's role in the conception remains far more mysterious. Quite likely, this complexity, this matter of the father being essential in the conception yet not intimately bound to the child, continues in a variety of forms as the son matures. One might suggest that it is symbolic of many father–son associations. The son realizes the essential nature of the father but cannot articulate the basis of this essential character. Similarly, the father appreciates his role in the conception of the son—some men even see their sons as their products or life work—but cannot always live out this felt sense of being essential. The result of this "essential-ness," conjoined with a peculiar form of distancing inherent in the period of gestation and often too in the period immediately following childbirth, is a tension, a strain, a push for intimacy on the one hand, a push for separateness on the other. Yet at some level the father and son believe that they are united. At some level, beyond their sharing of the same gender, lies the notion that they are one and the same, identical. This too contributes to the tension and the sense of guilt over one's individuation, individuality and identity. We spoke earlier of men, fathers and sons, finding their association to be almost club-like, tribal. Initiation into these club-like statuses often revolve around some ritual in which one man's blood is mixed with the blood of another man. In the case of fathers and sons, this mixing of the body's fluids in a sense has already been accomplished through the act of conception. Their encounter, inevitably, is consecrated by biology as well as by the psychological and sociological processes and routines that govern their lives.

The push for individual accomplishment, therefore, indeed the entire competitive struggle between sons and fathers, may find its origin in the earliest identification processes and the mysteries shrouding the very existence of both men. On the one hand the son must work at psychologically differentiating himself from his mother. He cannot, for example, return to the original psycho-biological relationship he once shared with her. But what exactly is he to do about differentiating himself from his father when their original "fusion" is so utterly unclear. In fact, when did he ever share the same sort of psycho-biological relationship with his father? The point is this: Much has been made in psychological, and particularly psychoanalytic literature, of the relationship between a boy and his mother. Much has been written, moreover, of the ambivalent manner in which a son beholds his father. There are also studies to be found of the attempt of one sex to differentiate itself from the other sex, the fear of androgyny, and related topics. What we know little about, however, is the association formed by father and son almost as a mutual pact, meant to assist them, as a partnership, in differentiating themselves not only from women, but from all other men of the same, former, and future generations. Said differently, it may well be the bond, the association in which men invest as they seek to ward off the anxiety of mortality and the confusion over their role in the conception and perpetuation of life. It is for these reasons that one is compelled to speak of the so-called spiritual nature of the relationship. Let us make the point in still another way.

What the life studies taken as a whole reveal goes far beyond the individual instances of strain, or search for tenderness and intimacy, or explications of hurt and frustration, cases of competitive envy or narcissistic assault. They speak to the fundamental existential nature of the bond inelucably holding men of different ages and generations together. The strains of being alive, the dread of the unknown, the terror of personal failure, the exhilaration of risk and challenge, manifestly individual experiences, on closer examination turn out to be essential constituents of the association made through biological as well as social psychological processes by fathers and sons. One can properly suggest that the relationship contains an element of the sacred in that it far transcends the mundane matters of everyday life. More significantly, life itself, its meaning and its purpose is embedded in the fabric defining the father–son bond. It is, in a fundamental sense, a universal bond because it contains elements that pertain to all people as they exist in the world through personal encounters. We are speaking, let us recall, not of two men, but of the boy and the man, the father and the son. (And who can utter these words without warding off the temptation to complete the religious triad!) The very words connote not merely another person—the father as father *to* the son, and the son as son *to* the father—but an association of these two people. And, despite the fact that each father–son relationship must by definition be unique, the universals quite likely of all father–son relationships must be captured in *each* of these unique and singular relationships.

The very meaning of being is encountered in the association we have been examining in these pages. One properly looks at the father–son bond, then, in life and death terms. It possesses this significance, and this dramatic urgency. The father who prepares for his son's life or competes with his son in some manner or other, or compensates his own felt sense of inadequacy by "living through" his son's achievements, is merely playing out the existential givens of the association. The two lives remain intertwined. The ontological givens and mysteries never recede, no matter how unique, individuated, autonomous, self-governing a father or son *believes* himself to be. Either many may choose not to be concerned with the fact of the association. Either man may choose to ignore the contribution of the other man's life to his own, but these actions are mere fictions, contrivances meant to help one achieve a sense of personal mastery and a temporary freedom from dependency and interdependency. Inevitably the truths of the association will be felt. It may take the death of the son or the father for the survivor to fully appreciate the magnitude if not the actual substance of the association, but each man, in the end, comes to learn of these truths. To not know them is to be unwilling to face the truths of one's being. Even more, it is to avoid looking face on at the man who bore you, or was born by you. And so it continues: like fathers, like sons.